AS THE SPIRIT LEADS US

If we really love
the Church,
the main thing we must do
is to foster in it
an outpouring
of the divine Paraclete,
the Holy Spirit.

Pope Paul VI
October, 1966

AS THE SPIRIT
LEADS US

Edited by
KEVIN AND DOROTHY RANAGHAN

PAULIST PRESS
PARAMUS, N.J. NEW YORK TORONTO

Nihil Obstat:
Very Rev. Msgr. William F. Hogan
Censor Librorum

Imprimatur:
✠ Thomas A. Boland, S.T.D.
Archbishop of Newark

March 1, 1971

The Nihil Obstat and Imprimatur are official declarations that a book or pamphlet is free of doctrinal or moral error. No implication is contained therein that those who have granted the Nihil Obstat and Imprimatur agree with the contents, opinions or statements expressed.

Library of Congress
Catalog Card Number: 77–152573

Cover design by Morris Berman

Published by Paulist Press
Editorial Office: 304 W. 58th St., N.Y., N.Y. 10019
Business Office: 400 Sette Drive, Paramus, N.J. 07652

Printed and bound in the
United States of America

Acknowledgment

The chapter entitled "Dynamics of the Prayer Meeting" by James Cavnar was originally published in slightly different form by Dove Books, Our Lady of Guadalupe Monastery, Pecos, New Mexico 87552.

Contents

Introduction

The public upsurge of the movement for charismatic renewal in the Catholic Church is approaching the fourth anniversary of its first rumblings. This movement is one of spiritual revitalization, at once deeply personal and socially engaging. Often referred to as a pentecostal movement, its energies tend to be concentrated in the double-edged thrust of continual personal conversion of life to Jesus as Lord and Savior, and an ever-ready desire to live and act as his disciples by the power-filled direction of the Holy Spirit.

Catholic men and women involved in this charismatic movement are thoroughly Catholic, firmly rooted in Scripture, the liturgy, spirituality and teaching of the Church. Unlike many of their counterparts in the classical Protestant pentecostal tradition, most of these Catholics are not inclined toward biblical fundamentalism or excessive emotionalism, and, further, they seem to be able to balance eschatological expectations with the concerns of socio-political involvement. Yet they constantly call attention to the need for all Christians to be aware of the reality and power of the Holy Spirit as the source of all successful life in Christ. The "pentecostals," as they are often called, cry out to brother and sister Christians of all denominations really to believe in, to expect and pray for, the life-giving action of God's Spirit on every level of human existence.

In 1969 we wrote *Catholic Pentecostals,* the first book of its kind, an historical and theological introduction to the movement for charismatic renewal in the Church. The historical sections of that book covered barely more than the first year of this new force in the Church. Since then, far from petering out, this movement has been growing quietly but steadily. Estimates of the number of Catholics involved in it vary considerably, ranging from 10,000 to 30,000. We know first-hand of several hundred prayer groups all across the United States and Canada. Regularly we hear of new groups in Latin America, in England, in New Zealand, or in Hong Kong. In June of 1970 approximately 1,800 Catholics, representing prayer groups from all over the United States, attended the fourth annual Catholic Conference on Charismatic Renewal in South Bend, Indiana.

As the Spirit Leads Us is not meant as a continuation of the history of our first book. It is rather a collection of essays, written by individuals deeply involved in this movement, reflecting upon aspects, directions, and implications of this renewal in the Spirit as the movement grows and develops within the Catholic Church. Here the reader will find ideas on worship, witness, ecumenism, and the present condition and future development of the Church, all formed and expressed from the charismatic perspective. Several articles on the formation of Christian community will also be found, and are, we believe, characteristic of all that the Spirit has been leading us to see and then to incarnate.

The Church is entering more fully into an age of community. Since Vatican Council II, we are increasingly drawn out and away from exaggeratedly individualistic prayer and piety and toward the vision of our common life within the body of Christ. Charismatic gifts are given for the common good, gifts given to one person for another, gifts given to serve the body of Christ, to build up community. In this way, in this time, tools have been fashioned for man to enable him to cooperate in that work which belongs to the Spirit of God, building and forming the people of God. Charismatic renewal runs at the heart of the renewal of the Church.

For Catholics within the movement, as well as for our Protestant brethren similarly involved in other denominations, we hope that these essays will provide some teaching and insight into what we believe to be a principal part of God's plan for us today. For our brothers and sisters in Christ who may be sympathetic or skeptical observers of this charismatic movement, we trust that this book will supply some measure of understanding.

Kevin and Dorothy Ranaghan

Baptism in the Holy Spirit

Dorothy Ranaghan

Four years ago, I saw a picture in a magazine that seared itself into my memory. It was a picture of an ordained minister holding in his hand a black, leather-bound edition of the Bible. But within the book he held, every reference to the Holy Spirit had been neatly scissored out. Line by line, passage by passage, chapter by chapter—all evidence of the Spirit of God had been removed. And what was left of that Bible was a shredded mass of paper. The tattered condition shocked me, not because this was shabby or irreverent treatment of the Word of God, but because there was so little left of the substance of that big book—just a line there and a page here. It was as if the very core of the book had been edited out, and what remained were fragments of the Word of God. That picture is stamped in my mind as one of the most graphic, vivid examples of the full truth and meaning of the Spirit of God.

And yet for most Christians, the Holy Spirit has been scissored out of their lives. If they allude to him at all, it is usually with grossly inadequate images and understandings of who he is and what he accomplishes in their lives. He is either a dove or a wind, perhaps he is even a "third Person," but rarely a Person with power, a

Person who is the moving breath behind the Word of God.

For example: About two years ago a very young, enthusiastic, and well-meaning priest came to visit me because he had heard that we were involved in something called a "pentecostal movement," and he was about to give a series of retreat conferences to a group of young people in the week preceding the feast of Pentecost. He wanted the retreat to be on the theme of the Holy Spirit. He asked me for some ideas, and I shared with him what we had begun to see the Spirit concretely doing for individuals and for communities. I must have talked with him for twenty or thirty minutes about the miracles, healings, and other power of the Spirit unleashed now in the charismatic renewal sweeping through the Catholic Church. But I'm not sure he heard, because when I finished, he said: "Yes, I see, but I still think the Spirit of the New Testament is like a spirit of enthusiasm, the spirit we get to accomplish any kind of task or project. It's like when we speak of 'spirit' in a pep rally for a football game, and that's the kind of spirit that accompanies us as Christians. On the Christian 'team' we've got spirit. We find joy in and through each other and that spills over into what we do."

That was going to be the sum and substance of his so-called pentecostal retreat. It was beautiful imagery. It is very nice to speak of the Holy Spirit as the enthusiasm in what we do, or the vague force that unites us as if we were a huge Christian pep rally. But the imagery and the idea itself are theologically off base. The power of the living God, the breath of the divine union of the three Persons who form the Godhead, possesses us; we do not possess him by some power of mutual complementation, acceptance and reliance. Our fellowship does not create "the Spirit" or "a Spirit," but fellowship itself is rather born of the Spirit. None of this is simply theological nitpicking. It is not refining fine points for the sake of disputation. We must ask ourselves: Is the Holy Spirit the moving force behind our Christian lives? Is he the only source of life and power on our Christian journey? Is he a Person who lives, acts and has characteristics that are recognizable?

If our answers to all of these questions are yes, then we are close to the truth of the Holy Spirit. That truth, that Person, is much stronger than a vague force that whips people up to make them feel good as they live the Christian life. The truth is stronger. It is because the Spirit of Jesus dwells in the Church that she is truly the body of Christ. Only because she is enlivened by the Spirit can the Church continue to celebrate the paschal mystery of Christ in Word and sacrament, making the fullness of redemption present and effective in each generation. Only because of the operation of the Spirit in the Church can any man become a part of Jesus, share in his sonship, and through him love and worship the Father. Only in the power of the Spirit can a Christian manifest the love of Christ to others, speak out in word and deed the good news of salvation and draw men to life eternal. The truth is that without the event of Pentecost and the ongoing reality of Pentecost there is no Church and there is no Christian life. Salvation without the coming of the Spirit would remain a mere historical event inaccessible to contemporary man.

The Baptism in the Holy Spirit

It was the realization of this truth about the Holy Spirit and what he is meant to be in the lives of the Christians of today that initiated and formed the springboard for the now thriving charismatic renewal in the Catholic Church. From its origin in the fall of 1966 in Pittsburgh to the hundreds of prayer communities now meeting regularly across North America, we have come to realize that the Spirit of God is for the Church today as he was for the early Church. The faith that would have us know this presence and power of the Spirit, and to expect it in our time and our day, is the faith that is poured out in this charismatic renewal. Miracles and healings, prophecies, visions and speaking in strange tongues— these realities, Christian realities of the charismatic renewal, have grabbed the focus of attention among many people who look to the renewal. These seemingly extraordinary manifestations of the Spirit are present and they are real, and they are given as gifts of God to serve his body. But it is the new, deep, and abiding faith that is the essential, most lasting result of the charismatic renewal of the Church and of the individuals who form this people of God.

The central experience which crystallizes and initiates this newness of life in faith is known as the baptism in the Holy Spirit. To be baptized in the Holy Spirit is an expression gleaned from the pages of Scripture. In the Acts of the Apostles we read that while Jesus was with his followers after his resurrection, "he charged them not to depart from Jerusalem, but to wait for the promise of the Father which he said 'you heard from me, for John baptized with water, but before many days you shall be baptized with the Holy Spirit. . . . You shall receive power when the Holy Spirit comes upon you; and you shall be my witnesses in Jerusalem, and in all Judea, and Samaria, to the ends of the earth.' After saying this Jesus ascended into heaven" (Acts 1, 4–5. 8).

According to these words of Jesus, the result of being thus baptized with the Spirit is the reception of power —power to witness to Christ, power to preach the Gospel effectively throughout the world. That is the purpose of Pentecost. The baptism in the Holy Spirit is a "pentecostal experience" in the sense that it calls forth, it sends forth, an individual with a newness and empowering of the Spirit in the same way that the first apostles were sent forth. The baptism in the Holy Spirit as we use the term has been poured out in the Church since the first Pentecost Sunday, and through every complete baptismal celebration it is still poured out today. Initiation into the body of Christ through baptism, confirmation and the eucharist confers the Spirit of God upon man, and as each one is filled with the Holy Spirit, so too the Church is filled with the Holy Spirit. As the body of Christ, she has already received all the gifts and fruits of the Holy Spirit. What this charismatic renewal seeks to do through prayer and by trusting in the Word of God is to actualize in a concrete living way what the Christian people have already received. It is an attempt to respond with radical faith to the Spirit who has already been given so that the fire of his life, gifts and fruits may be enkindled in the lives of the members of Christ's body. For us this "baptism" is neither a new sacrament nor a substitute sacrament; it is a prayer, similar to a renewal of baptismal promises, a renewal in faith of the desire to be everything that Jesus would have us be.

The phrase "baptism in the Holy Spirit" which comes from Scripture has been used also among pentecostal fundamentalists who don't have the sacramental theology necessary to relate it to baptism and confirmation. In the last seventy years in the pentecostal movement within the Protestant Churches the term has acquired the sense given it by those who first encountered it in modern times—a definite experience of the Person and work of the Holy Spirit in the life of the Church, followed by manifestation of the presence of the Spirit as detailed in the New Testament. For Catholics, this experience is a renewal, making our baptismal initiation as children now concrete and explicit on a mature level. It is in this sense that we speak of a baptism in the Holy Spirit.

To renew their baptismal commitment, to live concretely and fully in the Spirit of Christ, thousands of American Catholics have prayed to be baptized in the Holy Spirit. There is no set form or formula for this type of prayer. It can take place in small or large prayer groups, with a friend or alone, but always with Jesus. It takes place with the "laying on of hands" or without this gesture, at home, at school, at work, at Mass, in the car, but always in expectant faith. In fact, if any one thing characterizes pentecostal renewal among Catholics, it is not tongues, or singing, or prayer meetings; it is that they come to seek a renewal in the Holy Spirit in simple faith, and, having received the answer to their prayers, they begin to walk in the newness of faith.

The people involved in the charismatic renewal are basically men and women of new and richer faith. Faith, of course, is a gift of God, a grace, an unearned favor. It comes to one in the plan of redemption by hearing and believing the Word of God, by witnessing the life of the Word lived out in the lives of Christians, by seeing the results of faith in the beauty of those around us. The life of witness is the life of the Church. It is the lived-out proclamation of the good news of salvation. Through preaching-in-action, the Spirit draws men to God in Christ and the life of faith is born. When men of faith pray with expectation, Christ's answer builds up their faith. What is difficult for many Catholics is coming to grips with the meaning of real expectation. Expectation does not hope or say: "Maybe the Lord will answer"; expectation boldly and with confidence—not in ourselves but in the promise of the Word of God—claims, knows, and expects that the Lord will act.

A man may come to seek baptism in the Holy Spirit because he has seen and believed the work of the Spirit in the life of a friend. He then trusts Jesus in prayer and expects that the Lord will renew in him the gifts and fruits bestowed in baptism but not fully activated in a living way. In the answer to that prayer, Jesus often becomes more real to the believer. He is much closer, more present in one's life. He is not only at the right hand of the Father; he the risen Lord is really alive among the members of his body. This old belief becomes a new awareness, becomes really real to the believer. The relationship in faith between this man and the Father through Christ has been deepened, transformed, and has become the center of personal existence. It would be false to characterize this new-found faith-life as a purely emotional experience. Certainly human emotion is involved in any act of love, and people respond emotionally according to their temperament. But it seems better to speak of this new faith on the level of a penetration and all-encompassing awareness and conviction which involves the whole body-person with all of his human qualities in a response of deep commitment.

The Prayer of Faith

Is this trusting faith which radically believes in the present action of the Lord justified? Isn't it somewhat presumptuous? Doesn't it tend to tell Jesus what he should be doing? Not at all. After all, faith, like anything else, must be judged by its fruit. An evaluation of this new faith-life shows that Jesus is able to take the center and controlling reign in our lives, that there is an increase in the fruit of the Spirit and a deepened love of the sacraments, that there is a deepened growth of personal and communal spiritual life. The evidence in the lives of Christians to this prayer of faith should be justification enough. But it does not seem presumptuous to pray for the realization of what we know Jesus has promised to and bestowed upon his Church: the counsel, teaching, life and power of his Spirit. To pray for such a reality is simply to take Jesus at his word and accept

what is already there. There is an authoritative basis for
this type of faith in the Word of God. Sadly, however,
we must admit that many Catholics are ignorant of
Scripture. The more deeply our faith-expectancy is rooted
in the living Word of God, the more we can overcome
the sense of false humility that keeps us from claiming
the promises of Jesus.

Because we all know our own sinfulness and are
aware of our shortcomings, we may close ourselves to
receiving anything from God. We may feel unworthy.
That is healthy, because we *are* unworthy. We are unworthy of the spiritual gifts, we are unworthy of baptism
and the eucharist, we are unworthy of salvation and
God's love. We are unworthy of Jesus Christ. The fact is
that the Lord uses the unworthy, saves the unworthy,
loves the unworthy. Realizing that the gifts of the Spirit
as revealed in Scripture are promised to all the Christian
people and are meant to be exercised by ordinary men
and women can do a lot to open us to exercising them
ourselves.

In paragraph 12 of the *Constitution on the Church*
from the documents of Vatican Council II, we read: "It is
not only through the sacraments and the Church ministries that the same Holy Spirit sanctifies and leads the
people of God and enriches it with virtues. Allotting his
gifts to 'everyone according as he wills' (1 Cor. 12, 11), he
distributes special graces among the faithful of every rank.
By these gifts he makes them fit and ready to undertake
the various tasks or offices advantageous for the renewal
and upbuilding of the Church, according to the words of
the apostle: 'The manifestation of the Spirit is given to
everyone for profit' (1 Cor. 12, 7). These charismatic gifts,
whether they be the most outstanding or the most simple
and widely diffused, are to be received with thanksgiving

and consolation, for they are exceedingly suitable and useful for the needs of the Church."

Prayer for the baptism in the Holy Spirit is, most simply, prayer in expectant faith for our baptismal initiation to be existentially renewed and actualized. Our experience indicates that the Lord accomplishes the renewal in each individual in many different situations and in no specific form. Only one thing seems to be essential: an authentic request that is radical, open, and available to the answer that the Lord will send. The results of the prayer are remarkable indeed. For the individual, charismatic renewal turns him around in his relationship with Jesus and with the body of Christ and enables him to be more effectively a tool and a leaven and a source of love for others. He becomes fully aware that the force that guides him and enables him to live the life of Jesus is the power of the Spirit. From this new faith-relationship with Jesus, individuals and communities find themselves growing more deeply in the fruits of the Spirit. Love, joy, peace, patience, kindness, goodness, faithfulness, gentleness, self-control—all these characteristics of the life of Jesus himself become increasingly present and possible in the lives of charismatic Christians. All the characteristics of Christ we have read about in the epistle to the Galatians (Gal. 5, 22–23) and which we have sought—the love of Christ, mutual forbearance and concern, the lack of strife and contention within community—these become tangible and real through the baptism in the Holy Spirit. It can be like a foretaste of heaven. It is a vision of what the Christian life is meant to be. Faithfulness and cooperation with the Spirit are imperative, however, for this state of affairs to endure. The seed has been sown. The power has been given.

Gifts for the Common Good

But from the very beginning it has been clear that charismatic renewal is more than an experience for one isolated individual. True, an individual meets his Lord and becomes empowered with the Spirit in a new way, but the purpose of renewal has always been to set him forth for the common good to serve others. From the very beginning, along with the interior transformation, along with the new faith, along with the deepened experience and presence of the fruits of the Spirit in the life of the individual, has been the experience of the bestowal of the ministry gifts, the charismatic gifts of the New Testament of the Holy Spirit. These are bestowed on an individual not as rewards for an exemplary Christian life; they are in no sense earned; rather, they are poured out on a group of believers for the sake of building up the Church and for the purpose of facilitating the proclamation of the Gospel. They are simply tools for the body of Christ. A charism is a gift given for the common good. The specific spiritual gifts that seem to be most in evidence in this charismatic renewal, in this outpouring of the Spirit, are those listed in 1 Corinthians 12 by St. Paul: words of wisdom and knowledge, faith, healing, miracles, prophecy, discernment, speaking in tongues and interpretation of tongues.

Our highly differentiated, contemporary and technological Christian community is shocked to confront the reality of charismatic service. But the movement of the Spirit among us has effected a return to the primitive list of ministry gifts mentioned by St. Paul in his epistles. The return to the exercise of these gifts was not a man-made decision based on nostalgia for the "olden days." Few of us would have chosen these gifts of all the abundance the Lord offers his people. But the Lord in his sovereign will has poured out, in effect, a new Pentecost.

It seems wise to look beyond our will and plan and purpose, our ways of doing things, and accept the great will and plan and purpose of God for each of us and for his entire Church. His tools—these gifts given to us with which to serve others—because they are his work seem to be renewing and restoring the faith of his people.

Through these charisms the Christian proclamation of the good news of salvation is shown to be more than abstract theory or pious platitudes. The troubled, sick, and hungry men of this world are touched with peace, health, deliverance, and release. The victorious life of Christ becomes known in the now. Healing, discernment, miracles, prophecy—all these signs, manifestations, or demonstrations of the Spirit cry out to men as they did in the New Testament times: "Jesus is alive! Jesus works wonders! Jesus is the Lord!"

The gift of tongues, truly the strangest of these gifts, is a gift of prayer and praise that is, for many, the initial response to this action of God in them, serving as the threshold of a life of walking in the power of the Holy Spirit. It is the externalization of the interior work of the Spirit; therefore, on the level of corporeality, it makes the experience of the Spirit real. Once a person has yielded his tongue and his voice to the words the Lord gives him, once he has given his body-person over so radically to the operation of the Spirit, the power of this dynamic seems to flow tangibly and visibly through his life. Some denominational pentecostals hold that unless we speak in tongues we have not received the Holy Spirit. This is an unacceptable identification for us, since we know we have received the Spirit in baptism. But we urge all persons to pray for and to expect this gift as a consequence of having been baptized with the Spirit.

A new life of faith for the individual and for the community, the experience of the gifts and fruits of the Spirit, building up the Church and manifesting Christ to the world—these seem to be the results of renewing our baptism in the Holy Spirit. What is renewed in this experience is born in the waters of baptism and is nourished in the continual celebration of the death and resurrection of Christ as we gather at the altar. In itself the worship of the Church embodies on the level of human religious celebration the totality of the Christ-event. Everything that Christ's redemptive love has wrought is made continually present at Mass, in the sacraments, and in the Divine Office of the people of God. Yet no one of us, no one community of us, can apprehend or embody all of that reality. The paschal mystery is here among us, yet veiled in signs and rites. We proclaim it until the Lord comes to bring it all to completion. Thus this renewal flows from the liturgy; it is nothing which is not already celebrated in the official worship of the Church. It is but a deeper realization of that reality among the faithful. It is the actualization on the level of personal faith-in-action of the Christ-event we commemorate.

The baptism in the Holy Spirit is given by God to those who earnestly seek it. It is a deepening of the life of the Spirit, which is the very source of Christianity. It is an ongoing prayer of faith which claims, in full expectation, Christ's promise of "another counselor to be with you forever" (Jn. 14, 16). The work of the Spirit in this charismatic renewal touches at the very heart of any other renewal which the Church has undertaken. The truth of the charismatic renewal is grounded on the truth of the Holy Spirit.

The Holy Spirit, the enlivening, personal power of God, exists in the Church today not as the unseen member of the Trinity, not only as an intellectual light switched on in times of decision, not only as a strange symbol in religious art or an impersonal dove flapping feathered wings, but in the same dynamic and powerful way that he operated in the apostolic Church. He comes upon those who take Christ at his word and wait for the Spirit he will send. He comes with an array of gifts to build up the Church, to make her strong, and to enable her as fully as possible to be the great sacrament of Christ in the world.

Charismatic Renewal in the Church

Stephen B. Clark

Recently I had the experience of finding myself at a party, talking to one of the "pillars of the Church" in our parish (a university parish). We found ourselves talking about the incarnation, and I discovered that he had no real belief in Christ. He had a way of using certain Christian phrases in an ambiguous way, but he thought that Christ was only a great man, not God, and he justified his participation at the parish by the fact that Christianity stood for important human values. Less than a month later, I found myself at an Easter Mass and this same man was the lector and commentator. I was being led in worship at the greatest feast of the Church year by a man who did not believe in Christ.

Experiences like this are common, more common perhaps at universities than ordinary parishes, but they are becoming increasingly common all the time. Equally disturbing to me are conversations I have had with men who have now left the priesthood; or conversations with nuns who are struggling with "the meaning of religious life." For some seem to be complete strangers to God. While it is not true of all who are leaving religious life, some seem to be leaving the Church and Christ and not just their way of life. All over the Church, there seems to be a real problem with faith—a crisis of faith.

The number of priests and nuns who are leaving, the unwillingness of the young to consider the priesthood, the great numbers of college students and high school students who are drifting away from the Church or who frankly confess that the "institution" has less and less meaning for them, the swelling ranks of the "underground Church"—all these are symptomatic of what I might term a morale problem, a problem of growing lack of dedication to the Church structure. A major element in this morale problem (though not the only element) is the faith problem, because so often when I find myself talking to these "leaders" of the Church about Christ himself, I sense a real bewilderment, a confusion, sometimes even a resistance in their relationship with Christ. One seminarian told me he wanted to be a priest because "priests are the ones who determine the future of the structure." But he was not so sure that he believed in Christ. There may be a grave problem with the structure, but the more urgent crisis is one of faith.

At a conference at Notre Dame almost two years ago, a priest who described himself as a "conservative" said something to the following effect: "I have been attracted to the pentecostal movement because just at the time when I see the old institutions of the Church crumbling, I see God pouring out his Spirit in a new way, forming something new to restore the old." It is indeed striking that just at the time when we are facing a crisis in the Church, a crisis which involves a widespread crisis of faith, we should see so many people, priests, nuns and laymen of all ages beginning to experience in a new way the presence of the Holy Spirit and his work in their lives.

Pentecostal movement, charismatic renewal, movement of the Spirit—it does not matter what we call it. Something is happening in the Church today which seems to be one of the answers, potentially the most important answer, of God to the present situation. It is not the only, all-sufficient answer. The problems of the Church in our

age are complex. But if God himself is the source of the
life of the Church, the renewal in the life of the Church
can only come through a renewal in our contact with
God.

The significance of this charismatic renewal does not
merely concern the internal life of the Church, but it has
implications for the mission of the Church as well. It is
clear from the opening words of the *Constitution on the
Church* that one of the main motivations of Vatican
Council II was to preach the Gospel to all men more effectively. It is also true that one of the main reasons for
so much of the discouragement in the Church today
comes from her inability to make any impact on the
world, her inability to communicate the good news to
modern man. I had spent almost a full year talking to
one fallen-away Catholic college student about Christianity. He was trying to find out about faith in Christ,
and we had gone through much material with only a little
progress. Then I heard of the charismatic renewal. I
visited Duquesne and Notre Dame and some of the early
centers of the movement. After returning to town, I
simply told this student what I had seen and heard and
experienced. It was the same Gospel—but now added
was the witness of the things God had done that let him
see God was alive. It made a visibly greater impact on
him than everything I had told him before. The next
time I got together with him, I felt the Spirit leading me
to read the story of the prodigal son to him and especially
to stress to him the humility of the father and how he
just wanted his son back. Within a short space of time,
he turned to Christ again.

Such students, like most men of the world today, find
no interest in impressive institutions. They are not much
interested in finding "values" or an ethical system. But
if God is the kind of reality that they can encounter, they
want him. Men of all kinds, from university students to
ordinary workers, are eager for experience of the super-

natural. They will go after anything to find it—drugs, Zen, spiritualism, even satanism. If Christ is someone who can be experienced, if his Spirit will change men's lives, how much more ready will they be to consider Christianity and turn to Christ. If there is to be a renewal in the mission of the Church to the world, there must be a renewal in the personal experience of Christ and in the power of the Spirit.

The Church is in great need right now, and God seems to be doing something in the charismatic renewal which can meet much of this need. What is this renewal and what does it mean? Those of us who take a responsibility for the Church—bishops, priests, brothers, sisters, parish workers, lay leaders of all kinds—need to know how to respond to the charismatic renewal pastorally. We need first of all to understand what its pastoral implications are. God has entrusted us with a great responsibility, and we need to be attentive to discern how God is working in the Church today.

To say it simply, what is happening is a renewal in people's relationship with God. God is becoming more present to them, and he is doing more for them. The charismatic renewal involves a new experience of God. The initiation into this new experience of God is referred to as being baptized in the Spirit, and the central concern of the charismatic renewal is that a deeper, experientially vital relationship with God the Father, in his Son, through his Spirit, should be the norm of Christian life.

People have described the experience of being baptized in the Spirit to me in the following ways: "I can't exactly explain it. For the first time I just knew there was a God and that he was in me. I just knew, that's all." "It gave me a vital contact with God. It lasts." "I experienced a deep peace, deeper than I had ever known before. And I knew and still know that this is God." "I didn't experience anything at the time, but it changed my whole relationship with God for the better."

Others describe it in terms of the effects that they have seen from it. Most commonly described are a new sense of the presence of God, a new awareness of Christ, a greater desire to pray, an ability to praise God, a new desire to read the Scriptures, the Scriptures coming alive as the Word of God, a new eagerness to have others know about Christ, a new compassion for others and a sensitiveness to their needs, a new sense of peace and joy, a greater appreciation of the Mass and the sacraments, a renewed devotion to Mary, and an experience of spiritual gifts like tongues, prophecy, and healing.

From one point of view, these things are not so extraordinary. They are all part of the Christian life—standard parts of the Christian life. People know they should be there and have described the Christian life in those terms. How often children have learned the names of the gifts and fruits of the Spirit and all through their lives have been willing to state that these things are given in baptism and confirmation. And there is the key point. Many Catholics have known their doctrine well, and they accept it. If anyone asks them what happens to them at confirmation or what they have been given in communion, they will give the right answer. They will even argue the truth of it, and many of them would die for it rather than deny it. In other words, they believe it—as doctrine.

But on the other hand, how many Catholics would be disturbed if they could never honestly say that they had experienced anything of the Spirit's presence? Would it bother them to say that even though they "received the gift of wisdom," they were not aware of any change, and in fact they had never felt like God had taught them anything? How many Catholics who might say that they have "received Jesus" in communion or "been fed with the life of Christ" can also say that they experienced something through communion?

I don't mean to say that no Catholics have ever experienced anything of God's working. That is not the point. But what I do mean to say is that our faith is often not the kind of faith that expects to experience the results of what we believe. We have been prone to keep the doctrinal formulas, and when we experience no changes because of our Christianity we simply say that grace is invisible and we are sure it happened, or we reinterpret the statements. To say that God gives us the gift of wisdom means that yesterday we learned something wise from our next-door neighbor. Well, God does work through circumstances, but the "infused gift of wisdom" means that God is supposed to teach us directly, and *that* we should notice.

This brings us to a key to understanding this whole spiritual renewal: it is a renewal of faith. The charismatic renewal means that God does more for us. But God can do more only when we have a new faith, the kind that opens us to his working. The presupposition of the charismatic renewal today (as in all the charismatic renewals of the past) is an expectant faith, a faith that expects God to do what he said. With this kind of faith, it is intolerable to believe that I have the gifts of the Spirit and cannot see any change as a result of it. Christian doctrine cannot be just carefully preserved theory. It has to be a description of my experience. Faith has to be more than accepting the right ideas. It has to count on God to make good his promises in a way that I can know that he is real.

The phrase "being baptized in the Spirit" (or renewal of confirmation, or release of the Spirit) is only the term for a person's entrance into a new life with God, a life that involves a greater experience of God's presence and a faith of the kind that expects to see God at work. And the term "charismatic renewal" (or pentecostal movement) does not mean that there is a new Christianity or a new doctrine. It rather means a renewal in the working of the Spirit. From this point of view, there have been charismatic renewals before. The monastic movement in the 3rd and 4th centuries was a charismatic renewal. The Franciscan and Dominican movement in the 13th century was a charismatic renewal. At the heart of the Counter-Reformation was a charismatic renewal. These renewals involved renewal in the experience of the working of the Spirit, and they were marked by an authentic revival of the gifts of prophecy, healing, miracles, inspired preaching and inspired teaching.

At the core, then, this is what the pentecostal movement or charismatic renewal is—God entering more deeply, more experientially, into the lives of Christians, a renewal in faith. The central contribution which it has to make to the Church today, then, is a strengthening of Christian life at its source—contact with God. But there are a number of things involved in it which will be of real value to the life of the Church and which strongly reflect the concerns of Vatican Council II:

1. A renewal in worship (and, consequently, a renewal in liturgy). One of the results of being baptized in the Spirit is a desire to praise and worship God for his own sake, because he is who he is. The liturgical movement has done a great deal to renew the forms of worship, but we need a corresponding renewal in the spirit of worship. Unless someone is in the kind of contact with God that gives him a desire to worship God (and not just to relate with other people), there will be no authentic liturgical renewal; charismatic renewal provides this contact.

2. A renewal in the use of Scripture. A renewal of contact with God's Spirit means a renewal in our ability to listen to God. One of the most noticeable effects of being baptized in the Spirit has been the awareness it gives people that God is really speaking in his Word and they must be willing to change their lives because of what it says and desire to listen to it for guidance. The biblical renewal in the 20th century has been strongest

in the area of improving biblical scholarship and getting biblical forms accepted in prayer and in theology. But if it is going to revolutionize the life of the Church, it has to bring men to use the Bible in a day-by-day way to make contact with God, and this the charismatic renewal does.

3. A renewal in sacramental life. Once a person experiences God's activity in his life and once he begins to learn to have faith in God's promises, he usually has a new expectancy toward the sacraments and a new appreciation of their importance. The pentecostal movement among American Protestants has been in a very unritualized way a sacramental renewal in a segment of Protestantism (the "conservative evangelical" segment) that based its contact with God almost completely on hearing and accepting the Word of God. And among Catholics it is producing the deeper appreciation of sacramental action and the faith in it that Vatican Council II sought.

4. A renewal in apostolic zeal. From the experience of Jesus, and of what he does for a person, comes a desire to share the knowledge of the living God with others. Vatican Council II called for a missionary spirit, an evangelistic spirit, among all Catholics, but this is one of the areas of renewal in which there has been the least activity. The charismatic renewal has led many people to appreciate the need of others for Christ and to become willing to try to see that others find him.

5. Ecumenical renewal. From its very beginning the pentecostal movement in the Catholic Church has been ecumenically oriented. It has brought Catholics into contact with other Christians through a sense of common sharing in the life of the Spirit. And it has brought them into communication with a group of Christians who never spoke with Catholics on a Christian level before—members of the pentecostal denominations. Moreover, it has done this while at the same time bringing Catholics to a deeper appreciation of Catholicism and of the spe-

cifically Catholic contribution to the ecumenical movement.

6. A revival of the charismatic gifts (spiritual gifts). Through a deepening of contact with God and faith in God has come a much more widespread experience of the gifts of tongues, prophecy, healing, discernment of spirits, etc. (1 Cor. 12). These gifts are the workings of God to equip Christians for the service of God. They add a greater power to the work of Christians.

What I have mentioned above are all effects which have been noticed already as results of the charismatic renewal. These are the fruits it has borne. If just these become universal in the Church, they would revitalize the whole life of the Church. But there are a couple of other areas where it has the potential of making just as radical a renewal. Three have already begun to appear in some of the original communities within the movement: (1) a renewal in ministry in the Church—the work of the Spirit making the ministry more charismatic and diversified; (2) a renewal in preaching and teaching in the Church—gifts of preaching and teaching are badly needed today so that Christian truth can give life; (3) a renewal in living—Christians learning to live "in the Spirit" in every area of daily life, consistently.

What is the charismatic renewal (or the pentecostal movement), then? It is a strengthening of one dimension of the life of the Church—the dimension of the working of the Holy Spirit. It is a movement in the same sense that the liturgical movement is a movement. It is not at all organized. There is no way of telling who is in it and who is not with any kind of definiteness. But just as the liturgical movement is concerned with one aspect of the life of the Church (public worship), so the charismatic renewal is concerned with one aspect of the life of the Church (the working of the Spirit). And just as the liturgical movement is concerned with something so basic that it affects every aspect of Christian life and yet it is still only one dimension of the Christian life, the same is true with the charismatic renewal. It is possible to tell where the liturgical movement has reached by the way people worship together, the kind of piety they have. The same thing is true of the charismatic renewal. Where people have experienced the presence of the Spirit, where they have a desire for praise of God and for listening to God, where they expect to see God work through the charismatic gifts, there a charismatic renewal has begun to take root.

Pastoral Implications

The charismatic renewal has a great treasure to give to the Church today. But it also presents a pastoral problem to the Church today, both for those who are involved and for those who would not consider themselves part of it but who feel a responsibility for the Church. In this it is again like the liturgical movement. I can remember back to the days before the liturgical movement was widely accepted. Many pastors considered the "litniks" one of their chief headaches, and many laymen were intensely annoyed at the changes that liturgical enthusiasts wanted to make in "their" worship. On the other hand, those who were involved in the liturgical movement were annoyed at the obvious backwardness of the average parishioner who would not be open to the ways in which he could deepen his liturgical life. It is almost hard to remember how much of a battleground a minor liturgical change could be. It is easier to remember that there was a real difficulty in getting the "renewed" and the "unrenewed" to come together in oneness of spirit at the same Mass.

It is traditional to have such pastoral problems. But the most important pastoral problem is not the human relations problem, but the question: "Where does it fit in?" If it has something good to bring to the Church, how do I look on it? How do I make it part of the life of the Church? This is the same problem that was faced when Catholic Action groups first came along, when CFM first came along, when the Cursillo first came along. The charismatic renewal needs some pastoral thought. Its pastoral implications are many.

Perhaps the first and most basic point to be made is that the charismatic renewal is for everyone. It is a renewal in something so basic to Christianity that it should never be the preserve of a special group. Everyone should have experienced the kind of release of the Spirit which is involved in being baptized in the Spirit, and everyone should be experiencing the charismatic gifts.

When the liturgical movement came along, there was a temptation to assign it to special groups. Just as you had a Legion of Mary in the parish and a Holy Name Society, so you could have a Liturgical Society. You could perhaps give this group a Mass for themselves. But people were not interested in such a thing, and the less trouble that was caused by the liturgical group the better. It became clear, however, that the liturgical movement's concern was not with a special group, but with everyone. The liturgical movement was trying to strengthen a dimension of the Church that is so fundamental that it is for all.

The same is true of the charismatic renewal. The life of the Spirit is not for a few. It is for all. It should be a normal part of the Christian life to experience the presence of God, to see him working through us with charismatic gifts, to want to praise God, to want to bring others to Christ. It should be a normal part of our Masses, as it was in the time of the New Testament, the *Didache* and *The Shepherd of Hermas*, to have prophecy, tongues and interpretation, inspired teaching, singing in tongues, and even healing and miracles. The work of the Spirit should be much more manifest, much more widely experienced. It should be standard for Christian life.

Let me put this point another way. Right now we have a pentecostal movement in the Catholic Church. It has a name because there is a recognizable group of people fostering a special "thing," although most of the Catholic people are not involved in it. It is similar to what the liturgical movement was. But it is rare for anyone nowadays to talk about the liturgical movement (except at liturgical conferences). The term is mostly used in an historical sense, because there was a time when it was only a small part of the Church whose "thing" was the liturgy. We do not use the term "liturgical movement" now because the liturgical revival has been such a success. Everyone wants to be "liturgical" today.

We need to keep the goal in mind, because there is a tendency for something like the pentecostal movement to become a party within the Church, for people to want it to be just a special group. But it is my belief that the charismatic renewal is something which God has begun because he wants a deep spiritual renewal in the whole Church. Whatever we do, we must keep this in mind.

In the meantime, I can see four basic options which can be taken to give the charismatic renewal a place in the life of the Church:

(1) *A Kind of Spiritual Boost or Revival.* There is a strong tendency for the charismatic renewal to be approached this way. People flock to wherever there is a pentecostal prayer meeting or a pentecostal conference to "get the Spirit." Many people are prayed over. Most can testify to some sort of a spiritual boost. It has certainly made faith more of a live option for many people. But it is just a one-shot experience for them. They come once, or even a few times. They feel that something good has happened to them. And then they go back to life as usual—or almost as usual.

Approaching the charismatic renewal as a spiritual

boost takes a person only part-way. Being baptized in the Spirit is only an initiation into a fuller life of the Spirit. It takes some real effort and dedication over a period of time to learn about all the different workings of the Spirit and how to yield to them so that they become a regular part of our lives. Being baptized in the Spirit is not a magic experience that changes us completely. Rather it is an introduction to a relationship with the Holy Spirit, and he changes us. But he only changes us as we come to know him better and learn about him.

If the Holy Spirit is going to be able to change us, we need to gather together with other Christians who have been baptized with the Spirit and worship God together, trying to be more and more open to the presence of the Spirit. We need to be formed as a group by the Spirit, especially by his working through the charismatic gifts. It is only by being faithful to coming together "in the Spirit" that we can experience what a life in the Spirit really is.

In other words, if the charismatic renewal is approached as a kind of spiritual boost or revival, it will sooner or later die. Perhaps people will look back at it nostalgically. Perhaps it will be another "regrettable incident" to be cited in the future as an example of what might happen if things are allowed to get too far out of hand. But even if the Church is benefited, it will miss much of what God has in store for it.

(2) *The Complete Renewal of Parts of the Church.* This is one of the most desirable ways for the charismatic renewal to change the life of the Church. If a group within the Church (a community, a working group, even a parish) can as a whole accept the charismatic renewal, the charismatic renewal can become a part of the life of the Church very effectively. This is what happened with the group I was working with, and I have seen it happen with other lay groups working in the Church and with

some houses of religious. It leads to a real renewal in the life and work of these groups.

But there is a warning I have to express here. For a group to be renewed charismatically takes more than just having each individual baptized in the Spirit. The group as a whole has to change the way they live together or work together. They have to learn *as a group* to live in the Spirit. They have to learn to pray together in the Spirit, to receive guidance together in the Spirit, to be open to the different workings of the Spirit as a group. This can take a great deal of time and effort, because we have to open up slowly to the work of the Spirit and let him change us. But having a community of people who are really in the Spirit together is worth all the effort it takes.

(3) *The Creation of Small Prayer Groups.* This is perhaps the strongest tendency in the charismatic renewal today. All over the country little groups are being formed to come together to pray informally, open to the gifts of the Spirit. These groups are "pentecostal," and they answer a real need in the lives of the people who make them up. They allow thousands of Catholics today to share with others their lives as Christians in a personal way, a way that helps them to grow spiritually.

In many situations, small prayer groups will have to be the normal form of life for the charismatic renewal in the Church. Sometimes they will be the normal form because the lack of openness to charismatic renewal in a specific place will only make small prayer groups feasible. Sometimes they will be the normal form because for a while there will be little interest on the part of many people. Sometimes they will be the normal form because there is not enough leadership to sustain anything larger.

Although there will be many situations in which small prayer groups are all that are possible, something more is needed if the charismatic renewal is going to be able to make the impact it can on the life of the Church.

There is a need for larger communities. They are needed partly because small prayer groups have a difficult time surviving and remaining healthy if they are not part of a larger community. But they are also needed because more can happen and much of the work of the Spirit can only grow in a larger community.

There will always be a need for small prayer groups in the charismatic renewal. A large community does not eliminate the need for also having cell groups within itself. Rather, it depends on them if it is to be strong. But to think only in terms of small prayer groups when a larger community is possible would be to limit the effect of the charismatic renewal.

(4) *The Creation of Charismatic Christian Communities.* I want to talk about this option at some length, because it is more difficult to understand and to implement. It is also more important.

Let's look at the situation in my parish (which is fairly typical). We have about 6,000 adult Catholics. To serve these Catholics, there are nine Masses on Sunday, three each weekday, a number of chances for confessions, and then the usual special programs (convert instructions, marriage programs, CCD, etc.). I would not want to say that our parish is not a community in any sense of the word. But it is only a community in a very broad sense. The average parishioner comes to Mass only on Sunday, he finds a place in a church filled with people he does not know and who are a different group from the last group he went to Mass with the previous Sunday, and he takes part in a Mass which is "standard" for that Sunday (the Masses in our parish are fairly similar). This is most of his life in the parish. A few in the parish take part regularly in other activities. Our parish, for all the renewal it has undergone, is still a service station, providing Mass and sacraments for all who come at the stated times and other auxiliary services for those who need and want them.

Now let me take the community in our parish that is forming around the charismatic prayer meeting. The prayer meeting is fairly large (250 people each time), but it is still small enough for everyone to meet together each week. The average person comes together once a week with the same group at a meeting in which they can be formed as a Christian community together in an ongoing way. He soon gets to know others. He knows some other people there *because* they are members of that community (not because he knows them from someplace else and they just happen to be at the prayer meeting). Each prayer meeting he takes part in is responsive to the state of the community at that time. He feels a real sense of interaction among the members of the community and a sense of identification with this group of people as a whole. Moreover, if he has been coming very regularly, he will find himself drawn into a number of other meetings for formation, apostolic projects and social events, none of which involve all the members of the prayer meeting, but all of which are in a real sense outgrowths of the community.

One way of stating where the difference lies is that the "pentecostal" community in our parish is a community in the way the early Church had communities, while the parish is not. The prayer meeting functions much the same way as the early Christian assemblies—as the gathering of a community where one group of people could be formed as a community of Christ. Moreover, because it is a real community, out of the prayer meetings grow many activities which give the community real impact on the lives of those who are a part of it.

In modern Catholic thought about pastoral realities, it is becoming more and more common to appreciate the significance of the Christian assembly and of communities of the type I am describing. It is part of the motivation for such experiments as the San Miguelito project, the floating parishes, and many of the continental model parishes. If we are going to recapture the life of the early Church, if we are going to have a Church which plays a vital part in the lives of her members, we are going to have to find a way of forming communities. And by "communities" I do not mean just primary groups, small groups. I mean larger groups (between 500–1,000) which really function as communities and out of which small groups can grow. My "parish," in other words, should be composed of six to ten smaller "parishes."

Now I am in a position to state more clearly what I mean by the fourth option (the creation of charismatic Christian communities rather than just the creation of small prayer groups). The goal of the charismatic renewal (whenever possible) should not be simply to form small groups of Christians for prayer in the Spirit, but to form full Christian communities. That means growing in a number of areas beyond that usually found in prayer groups. It means having regular teaching in Christian life, both at the main meeting and outside of it. It demands real emphasis on Christian services as well as prayer (and I don't mean that everyone in the community should be working on one apostolic project, but that everyone in the community should find his participation in the community leading to some definite Christian apostolic responsibility). It means that there must be some ministry (leadership) in the community. And, personally, I believe it also means that sooner or later the full eucharistic worship has to be integrated into the meeting of the community. In other words, what is needed are small churches.

I know that what I just said has a vaguely schismatic or heretical sound. I do not mean it to, but I don't know how to say it strongly enough and not have it sound that way. The Church needs such communities; Christians are dying for lack of such communities. I am not proposing that the charismatic renewal lead to Catholics splitting off from the Catholic Church to form new sects but that they build these communities within the Catholic Church as a new form of parish life. What is happening in our parish as a result of the "pentecostal" community is what should be happening for every Christian.

A logical question a person might ask here is: "Well, why do you need the charismatic renewal to do that? We could form large parishes into small Christian communities without the charismatic renewal." And the answer is: Of course we could. The idea of building smaller Christian communities is not particularly "pentecostal," and it could be done with or without the charismatic renewal. It is just good pastoral sense. But even an ideally structured community needs the full working of God's Spirit if it is going to be a living Christian community. When we think about pastoral renewal in the Church, we should be aiming at the formation of charismatic Christian communities (and not just charismatic prayer fellowship or non-charismatic communities).

I want to qualify even that. I don't think our aim should be described as forming "charismatic Christian communities." We do not want communities that are "specializing" in the Holy Spirit any more than we want communities that are specializing in the liturgy or specializing in social action or specializing in evangelism. We want full Christian communities, communities in which every dimension of Christian life is fostered as fully as possible. When we build a community, it should be a community in which all of Christianity is recognized, valued and encouraged. We should not get together to have our Thursday night devotion to the Holy Spirit. We should be getting together to build a body of Christ. And if it is a true body of Christ, each member should experience the presence of the Spirit in his life and the whole community should experience all the charismatic gifts (including tongues, prophecy, healing, miracles, etc.).

One of the greatest dangers in the Church today is a certain type of specialization. People are experiencing the need for community, and so they form communities with others around some special "thing." Their "thing" may be social action or it may be interpersonal relations or it may be the Holy Spirit. They have community, but their community is specialized. It is not open to the fullness of Christianity. And so we find ourselves in the paradoxical position, for instance, of having Christian communities where all a person can do is talk about social action, not about prayer, and vice versa.

There seem to be two basic options of how to go about forming full Christian communities. The first and most common is the "floating parish" idea. In many cities, Catholics are forming small communities around their Sunday liturgies apart from the parishes. Often these floating parishes turn out to be specialized communities, not full communities, but they are still pointing out one way in which real communities can be formed. One way of following the proposal which I am making might be to form charismatic floating parishes (floating parishes which include the charismatic dimension of Christianity too).

Personally, I think there is a better course, because the result of forming a floating parish is the abandonment of the present parochial structure. Most of the Church lives in the present structure, and therefore it would be better if dedicated Christians did not have to leave it. We have to live through a stage of evolution— evolution from the present parochial structure to a new parochial structure. This is not the place to suggest how that evolution can take place, but the charismatic renewal should lead to Christian communities forming within our present parish, as an integral part of it. I think this is what is happening at our parish, and I hope it continues. Not only do the Catholics at our prayer meeting come regularly to the prayer meeting, they also come regularly to the liturgy, especially to the two community Masses we have. Some of the apostolic projects they work on and the study groups they take part in are made up exclusively of people from the prayer meeting, but most of them are parish projects. In other words, the "charismatic community" is beginning to provide willing workers for the parish, most of whom were indifferent members of the parish or had fallen away before having been baptized in the Spirit.

It is more difficult to keep a state of integration than to start a new community. It would be easier to form a floating parish than to form a Christian community within a parish. A floating parish provides greater freedom to operate. Granted, there are a number of human relations problems that come from having a community within a parish. But if the contribution of those who are "pentecostal" is going to be saved for the Church, and if everyone is going to be kept in dialogue with one another, the human relations problems will have to be worked through.

What I have proposed leaves out of consideration another whole area: the ecumenical aspect. I have been talking about charismatic renewal within the Catholic Church, and yet it is very common to find groups of Christians meeting together in "charismatic communities" across denominational lines. This has, in fact, been one of the best features of the whole charismatic revival—its ability to bring Christians of the most diverse backgrounds together in oneness of spirit.

The ecumenical contact should continue. This is something God wants. But we must have it continue in such a way that it fosters a charismatic renewal in all the Churches. There is a great deal of room for ecumenical meetings without destroying the focus of forming full Christian communities within the parish. Our main prayer meeting (predominantly Catholic but including many Protestants) has given rise to a number of smaller prayer meetings made up mostly of people who come to the big prayer meetings too. Many of these small prayer meetings are in university dormitories where it is very natural, advantageous in fact, for Christian students of any denomination to meet together and to work together to bring other students to Christ. Two other prayer meetings are mainly made up of people in churches other than the Catholic parish. In other words, while our primary direction has been the renewal of the Catholic parish, the charismatic renewal has led both to ecumenical cooperation and renewal in local Protestant church groups.

It should be a major concern of those who have leadership responsibility within the Church to find the place for both the charismatic renewal and the communities arising within it which will make the greatest contribution to the life of the Church. Too often groups of Christians have become alienated from the institution of the Church. The result is underground churches, groups of Christians who are almost militantly unwilling to contribute positively to the institutional Church. The same could happen with the charismatic renewal. As it is, most Catholics who have been touched by the charismatic renewal have a deep desire to be loyal Catholics and to contribute to the life of the Church. It is the encouragement, openness and wisdom of the leaders in the Church which will make all the difference.

But we need to take our pastoral responsibility seriously for more than negative reasons. It is not just that we do not want a new group of people to join the ranks of the alienated; more importantly, if God is giving his Spirit in a new way, it is for a purpose. The Spirit of God is given to form and build up the body of Christ. Today, the Church is in great need of renewal in the power of God. We need to learn to form all the life and work of the Church "in the Spirit." Our responsibility for the Church means a responsibility to draw all the strength possible from each of his workings for the renewal of the whole Church.

The Nature of the Prayer Meeting

Kevin M. Ranaghan

Perhaps the principal public manifestation and result of the charismatic renewal in the Church today is the phenomenon of the prayer meeting. Wherever people are receiving the baptism in the Holy Spirit, realizing their lives transformed through deeper participation in the life and power of the Holy Spirit, one of their first desires is to enter into a fellowship of prayer with other Christians sharing the same experience.

Prayer meetings come in all sizes and shapes: some are quite large, numbering in the several hundreds; others are quite small, perhaps only of three or four people gathered together in a living room. More normally, the prayer meeting consists of a group numbering between twenty and thirty persons. Most of the groups in our experience are made up predominantly of Catholics. However the ecumenical aspect of the charismatic renewal in the Church today has been evident from the very beginning of this outpouring of the Holy Spirit among us. Many groups may be characterized as so ecumenical that no one denomination or spiritual tradition predominates at the meeting.

In some principally Catholic prayer groups, the percentage of Protestants in attendance is quite large, while in others it is quite small, or non-existent. At an average prayer meeting one is apt to find people from every walk of life as well as from every social, economic, and educational level. These factors of course are variable, depending upon the size and place of the gathering. But it is generally agreed that a major characteristic of the pentecostal renewal among Catholics is that it cuts through all levels of Catholic society. It is neither a student nor an intellectual group, neither a middle-class nor a lower-class movement. People from every type of background participate very freely with few barriers of class distinction remaining. It is often at the local regular prayer meeting that people attracted to the charismatic renewal in the Church receive their first introduction to it and experience what the Lord is doing among us today. In addition, these meetings provide the normal and perhaps principal means of continuing association and fellowship among those who have received the baptism in the Holy Spirit, so that, through the assembly, what they have already received may be nurtured, sustained, and given continuity in terms of day-to-day living.

The various service gifts of the Holy Spirit which are so prominent in the charismatic renewal in the Church are expected to be in operation at the local regular prayer meeting. Because of this heightened faith, they usually do take place within that context. Furthermore, both observers and critics of the movement tend to make their judgments and evaluations of its worth on the basis of the prayer meeting itself, rather than on the basis of the working of God, the new life in Christ, the fruits of the Holy Spirit, appearing in the individual lives of those who have received the baptism in the Holy Spirit.

Participants in the charismatic renewal in the Church, on the other hand, seem to place a variety of values on the regular group prayer meeting. For those who are young in the Spirit, new to the pentecostal movement, the prayer meeting provides a place of faith-filled fellowship to which they can come to see the continuing action and grace of God in their individual lives, to seek the fulfillment of their personal needs, to give their witness of what the Lord is doing with them personally to the other members of the body. The prayer meeting for them is a time of personal worship and witness and service to others in the context of a shared experience. In many places, however, where the charismatic renewal has been taking place for several years, and where the Lord has been bringing about a maturity among those baptized in the Holy Spirit, there is a growing realization of the necessity to move beyond the casual association type of prayer meeting to a prayer meeting which embodies and expresses no longer the lives of individuals who have accidentally come together but the life of a solidly committed Christian community. The individual experience of the power of the Holy Spirit leads to deep personal commitment to the other members of the prayer group.

Casual association develops into deep friendship and mutual care in Christ. In fact, strong dimensions of community life—sharing the totality of Christian experience with each other through mutual commitment to Christ and to each other—emerge, and then the prayer meeting takes on a new dimension. It becomes a site of the encounter between the community and God. Very conscious of belonging to each other as brothers and sisters in the body of Christ, the members of this type of prayer group see and experience in the prayer meeting a place of corporate worship, corporate witness and corporate ministry. They see it also as the place where the Lord, by the power of his Spirit, moves among them as a whole, not only meeting individual needs, but giving direction to the life and ministry of the whole body. For all these reasons it is necessary to examine the nature and the role of the prayer meeting in some depth.

Is the prayer meeting a novelty, an exercise in group dynamics or sensitivity, or the result of the influence of contemporary group psychologizing? Is the prayer meeting a type of worship previously foreign to Catholicism, and to Catholic spirituality? Is it perhaps a creation of Protestantism which is making inroads into Catholicism? Or is there something about the prayer meeting that makes it essentially Catholic, deeply rooted in the Catholic tradition? These are some of the questions we will discuss here.

Dialogue Between God and Man

One way of describing the human phenomenon of religion is as an attempt on the part of man to approach God, to encounter God, to establish a relationship with him. In every human society, whether primitive or sophisticated, a chief characteristic is always its inner drive and impulse to appropriate to itself, and to perpetuate within itself, the power of life. Whether we are talking about the fertility religions of the ancient world which sought to obtain the powers of fecundity and reproduction for the community's harvest or flock, or whether we are talking about the totemism or animism of tribes in Africa or the Americas, we can say in general that what the group really wants to do is to approach, to befriend the source of life, and to receive from that source the perpetuation of life within itself.

What we are discussing here as a human phenomenon is the movement from man toward God, the effort, the approach, the program on the part of man to get in touch with the "source of his life," to placate the deity, to implore the help of "the gods," to worship the God who is seen above all as the ruler, the powerful one, the source of continued existence. We, however, who are the heirs of the Judaeo-Christian tradition are not bound to approach God simply from the point of view of natural religion and our own striving. Rather, we speak of our faith from our knowledge and experience of it as revealed religion. For us, man is not limited to approach some vague power whom he calls his God. But, rather, the true God himself has revealed himself, has spoken to us, has approached us and has taken the initiative in establishing a relationship with us. What gives the Judaeo-Christian tradition its unique quality is the fact that within its ambit God has truly revealed himself to man and has enabled man to respond to him. And thus it is possible that a dialogue, a personal relationship, can exist between God the creator and man the creature.

The creation of the universe and everything in it is in itself a revelation of God. The high point of that creation is the family of man, the human race. Just by his very existence within human society, man hears, in the broadest sense of the word, the voice of God. The whole of creation is the product of God's Word in action. According to Scripture the Word of God was God's agent in bringing the cosmos into being. God spoke his Word and it was done, so that through the Word of God, through the Person of the Word of God, whom we now understand to be the second Person of the Trinity, all things were made. This we affirm in reciting the Nicene Creed when, speaking of the Word, we say "through whom all things were made." Therefore, at the high point of creation the Word of God creates and evokes a people. The creation of mankind, the creation of the human family, is the work of the Word. And the people respond to the Word in creative action, most basically in the process of accepting and living life. Fundamentally, humanity is a people formed by the Word of God, created by the Word of God, and meant to respond to God through the Word which it hears.

Moving beyond the level of creation we come once again into the area of the Judaeo-Christian tradition, of revealed religion, of God revealing himself by speaking to men. Just as through the action of the Word God created us, from the beginning of salvation history God has communicated himself and his life to us directly, by speaking his Word to us. What we know of God by revelation we have learned only through God's Word coming to us and speaking to us. Just as the high point of the creative activity of the Word was the creation of the human family, so also the Word of God now speaking to us in revelation (and as recorded in Sacred Scripture) always seeks to form a people who are to respond, to speak back to God, to dialogue with God particularly in terms of praising him, worshiping him and confessing him to be God. Thus the people formed by the Word share in God's life as they live out their own lives by entering into a personal relationship with him.

This point is crucial. In the process of revelation, in the process of God's saving action in history, God speaks his life-giving Word to men. The people formed by the Word are formed by it into his people, into his community. In hearing the Word and being formed by it, they are led to respond to God and thus enter into the relationship to which he has called them. We might say this: the Word of God comes to form a people to such an extent that God has never spoken to individuals as such, has never spoken to an individual just for the purpose of speaking to him as an individual. Rather, God speaks to and through individuals in order to form his people, in order to form his community. Therefore, the Word of God is always calling individuals to come together, to form a people, to assemble in order to hear, to ratify and to respond to his life-giving Word.

God's Word in History

An idea of this saving activity of God's Word is seen in the outline of salvation history. Salvation history may be said to begin with God's revelation of himself in his call to Abraham. God revealed himself to Abraham and invited him to enter into a relationship of faith with him. And God promised that he would be Abraham's God and that through Abraham he would build for himself a people, that he would create his people and that these people would share his life. The Word of God came to Abraham, and Abraham heard the Word, the Word which promised the people, and Abraham responded to the Word in faith and accepted God's covenant, the testament that he offered him.

The relationship that was created by the action of the Word between Abraham and his God is called a covenant relationship. This covenant relationship, expressed in God's promise to Abraham and in Abraham's fidelity to God, became the key factor, became that which in fact distinguished Abraham's family, his people, from everyone else. They became the covenant people.

Several hundred years later, around 1250 B.C., this process of God speaking by his Word in order to form his people was repeated in the revelation by God of himself to Moses. The descendants of Abraham, Isaac and Jacob along with many other people from a variety of backgrounds were in forced labor in Egypt. God revealed himself to Moses and called him to form these scattered groupings into his people. In revealing himself to Moses God told him to bring these masses out of Egypt, principally so that they might come out to worship him at his holy mountain. Moses spoke the Word of God to the people and to the Egyptians, and as a result he was able to lead the people out to God's holy mountain, Sinai, where they worshiped him.

There on Sinai, the Word of God came to Moses and expressed the great promise of the covenant relationship which God wished to have with his people: "I will be your God and you will be my people." The covenant relationship is established by the Word—between God and the people under the headship of Moses. Israel, the people of God, was born. In the scene as recorded in Exodus 24, we see that the people assembled to hear this Word of God, and that, on hearing it, they responded, they affirmed it, they ratified it, and as a result they began to live life with God.

From that time forward at every high point in the history of Israel we find a repetition of the same pattern. God continues to communicate with his people by his Word; his Word comes forth from him in order to form and mold and shape his people and in order to lead his people to praise and worship him and thereby to share his life. This is true in the establishment of the kingdom for the people of Israel, as it is true in the age of the prophets who have such an important place in the history of Israel. Over and over the Word of God comes to the prophet and is spoken through him in order that the people might again hear the Word of God and turn from their wicked ways and reaffirm the covenant relationship that had been established at Mount Sinai through Moses.

An outstanding example of this process is the event of the deuteronomic reform under King Josiah in the year 622 B.C. when under his leadership there was a real revival of the covenant religion among the people of Israel. The law of the covenant was expanded upon and made more relevant to the people. And there is in 2 Kings 23 the scene where all the people of Israel assembled to hear the reading of this law, to hear the reading of God's will. After hearing the Word of God the people ratified it anew, radically renewing their covenant relationship with God. Once again the Word spoken from God had come into the midst of the people assembled, had formed the people and led the people closer to God in worship.

The convocation at Sinai was the first great assembly of Yahweh in the Old Testament, and that of Josiah was the second. The third great assembly of the whole people that marks a turning point in the history of Israel is found in Nehemiah 8, 17 and 13, 1. Here is described the end of the Babylonian exile and the return of the people to the devastated Holy City, Jerusalem. In all that ruin they still had one thing, the Word of God, now embodied in the Bible of the scribes. The scribe Esdras called the assembly and had the Bible read to the people. The people ratified it and Esdras himself led a great prayer of thanksgiving, praising God for his past deeds and looking forward to the future fulfillment of God's Word in, through, and for his people.

The work of God's Word in salvation history was to form God's covenant people. The terms of the covenant— "I will be your God and you will be my people"—were lived out in a quality called *hesed*, covenant faithfulness, as each, God perfectly and the people imperfectly, kept the terms of this relationship. This whole process is recorded and transmitted in Sacred Scripture, which is seen to be the written expression of the Word's action and the people's faith response. The people's response was their life lived faithfully to God, epitomized in their worshiping assemblies. At the heart of these assemblies was always the proclamation of the Word of God and the hearing of and response to the Word of God.

Jewish Assemblies

Up to this point we have been establishing a general principle about the way God deals with men. Throughout salvation history, as we have seen so far, God sought to give men life by sending his Word to speak to and to create his people, by sending his Word to call his people together and to speak words of life to them. He wished to evoke from them a response of faith and worship which would enable them to enter into life with him and thus to experience redemption.

Beyond this we should look at the forms of some

assemblies convoked around God's Word in the history of Israel. In the beginning of the period, when Israel dwelt as a tribal confederation after crossing the Jordan River under the leadership of Joshua, up until the time of Kings David and Solomon, the worship of Israel was epitomized in three annual festivals which were held at local shrines or sanctuaries. Three times a year, the people went up to a local sanctuary to worship God. One occurred in early spring, at the time of the beginning of the grain harvest, to celebrate and to commemorate the passing over of the people out of Egypt and their formation as the people of God; the second was at Pentecost, at the end of the grain harvest period, to celebrate life in the law and in the Spirit of God; the third was in the early fall at the time of the fruit harvest, during the Feast of Tents or Booths, to commemorate the time when the fathers of Israel pitched tents in the desert as God was leading them to the promised land. Three times a year, then, the people went up to the ancient local sanctuaries, and there they assembled around the Word of God which re-created the events of their salvation in their midst. There they celebrated and responded to the Word of God by worshiping and praising God who had saved Israel. In these sanctuaries the praise of the people was epitomized in the sacrifices of the people.

At a later stage in the history of Israel, after the establishment of the kingdom, the Jerusalem temple was built, the place of worship *par excellence,* meant to replace all the local sanctuaries and to be the central location where the people of God were to assemble to hear the Word. In the temple, from this time onward down until the time of the Babylonian exile, the people of Israel came three times a year to celebrate the great festivals around the Word of God. Here we find the elaborate priestly cult of sacrifice through which the people assembled to respond to the Word of God in regular sacrifices during the morning and late afternoon.

Indeed the people were most intensely God's people when, gathered in Jerusalem, they assembled together for the celebration of a great feast and sought spiritual renewal by listening to the Word of God and responding in praise and sacrifice.

Even later in the history of the Jewish people, a new center for the assembly of God's people sprang up. During, and especially after the time of the Babylonian exile, we find the origin and then the rapid development of a new type of religious institution, the synagogue. The word "synagogue" has the same basic meaning as our word "church"; it means simply the assembly. During the time of the Babylonian exile, when the Jews were away from the Jerusalem temple and the regular priestly worship of the temple could not take place, the Jews had a need to assemble to hear and respond to the Word of God. Furthermore, about the same time in their history, a condition arose which became characteristic of Judaism from then on. Jews were to be found not only in Judea, not only in the area of Palestine, but also scattered thoroughly around the then known world—from Alexandria in northern Egypt, through all of Syria, Persia, Asia Minor, Greece, Italy, even as far as Gaul and Spain. From this period on local communities of Jews were found almost everywhere. This phenomenon is often referred to as the diaspora, the scattering. For Jews who for one reason or another lived away from Jerusalem, there could be no temple worship—at least no regular temple worship—unless they made an effort to get up to Jerusalem for one of the major festivals. Still, in terms of the demands of normal religious life, there was a need for another place to assemble to hear and respond to God's Word. Thus occurred the development of the local synagogue as a place where the Word of God could be spoken among the people, could be commented upon, studied and contemplated. It became the place where the Word of God could call together God's people and evoke from them the response of praise and worship which would perpetuate among them a life-saving relationship with God.

The synagogue did not develop as an institution foreign to or in opposition to the Jerusalem temple, but it attempted to be a kind of local station where the activities of prayer and worship were carried on in conjunction with the activities in the Jerusalem temple. For example, every synagogue was built so that the assembled congregation was facing toward Jerusalem, toward the temple, toward what was believed to be the intense dwelling place of the *shekinah Yahweh,* the presence of the Spirit of God among his people in the Holy of Holies. Furthermore, the daily services in the synagogue at morning and at evening were held at the same times that the morning and evening sacrifices were being offered by the priests in the temple, in union with them. However, instead of sacrifice, which could be performed only by the Jerusalem priesthood, the heart of the synagogue was the reading of, the commenting upon, and the responding to the Word of God. The center of synagogue activity was the proclamation of the law and the prophets.

It is extremely important for us to realize that from the end of the Babylonian exile, and with increasing emphasis down to the time of Jesus, the normal and regular matrix of Jewish worship was the synagogue. The synagogue was the normal site, the regular place in each village, even in Judea itself, where God's people assembled and worshiped the Lord. The synagogue service normally consisted of prayers of praise and blessing God for all his goodness among his people, of listening to the Word of God, and of hearing it expounded by the rabbi, which led then to a response of intense blessing of and thanksgiving to God and prayers for the fulfillment of his plan among his people.

The synagogue and its piety became the dominant factor in the formation of Jewish piety. From the experi-

ence and the teaching of the synagogue developed the
whole system of daily prayers of blessing which were
meant to be recited by the pious Jew throughout the
day, so that from the worship of the synagogue flowed a
state of more or less continual prayer and reflection on
the goodness of God. Also from the synagogue was seen
to flow the good works of charity and almsgiving, as well
as such qualities as honesty and upright family life. The
influence of the synagogue stimulated contemplation of
the Word of God and reflection on God's law and its
meaning. We cannot overemphasize the fact that at the
time of the emergence of Christianity, even though the
temple cult was in full swing, the synagogue was the
normal place of the experience of worship for both Jesus
and those he attracted. The normal Jewish religious experience was synagogue-centered rather than temple-cen-
tered. The synagogue of each village repeated for the
local congregation the same great event of God's revelation: God speaking to them by his Word, and thus making them a people, leading them to respond to him in
praise and worship and thus to deepen their life in him.
Just as God had revealed himself to Abraham, to Moses,
and to the prophets in order to form his own covenant
people, so now God revealed himself and spoke by his
Word in the midst of his assembly at the synagogue of
the local place. Here the people encountered God through
the written Word proclaimed. Here the people came to
know the Lord their God and to respond to him in
psalms, hymns and prayers of praise.

The Christ Event—The Living Word Made Flesh

Throughout salvation history God had been continually forming his people by speaking his Word to them.
In the fullness of time God spoke (his Word) definitively
in the incarnation of his Word, in Jesus of Nazareth. Jesus

is the living Word of God, the Word incarnate, the Word made flesh: the second Person of the Trinity, who took upon himself a human nature. In the incarnation of Jesus, in the whole process of his incarnation, life, death, resurrection and sending of the Holy Spirit, God says ultimately and finally everything he has to say to man. So we read in the opening verses of the Epistle to the Hebrews: "In many and various ways God spoke of old to our fathers by the prophets; but in these last days he has spoken to us by a Son, whom he appointed the heir of all things, through whom also he created the world. He reflects the glory of God and bears the very stamp of his nature, upholding the universe by his Word of power."

The entire Christ-event, the whole purpose and plan and effect of the life and death of Jesus, was to definitively establish the perfect dialogue between man and God. Jesus as man is the first and only human ever to respond perfectly to God, ever to perfectly fulfill in his personality the covenant relationship which is man's salvation, man's life with God. The result of this is the new covenant, the new creation, the new people of God, a new race under the headship of the new Adam. In Jesus of Nazareth, God's Word speaks fully, clearly, and effectively so that men are able to respond in praise and thanksgiving through the living Word, through Christ himself. Thus men really do share God's very life, are truly saved, redeemed, and filled with the Holy Spirit as had never been possible before. In the Christ-event the Word came among men and accomplished in the person of Jesus Christ what the Word had always been about: a new people of God, a body of Christ where men can share in his perfect relationship with the Father, which is eternal life.

The Christian Assemblies

How was all of this celebrated in the life of the primitive Christian community after the outpouring of the Holy Spirit on Pentecost? The early Church duplicated the pattern we observed in the Old Testament and Judaism. According to Acts 2, the new Christians who heard the Word, repented, were baptized and received the gift of the Holy Spirit, entered into regular meetings. They came together as a people to pray, to receive the teaching of the disciples, and to celebrate the breaking of the bread. In this assembly Jesus the Word of God is personally present, forming this new people, this body of Christ, as well as leading their response of worship. The Word leads their worship to the throne of the Father.

Furthermore we have the practical testimony of Saint Paul in 1 Corinthians 12–14 where he teaches how the Christian people came together as a body, united as the various parts of the body are united to each other. By the power of the Holy Spirit, we are as bound together as the sinews, bones, and organs of the human body. Thus the concrete solidarity of this people is most intensely present, says St. Paul, as they in fact assemble together. There is, however, an added dimension: the assembly is the setting for the operation of the ministry gifts of the Spirit. Especially for the purposes of the assembly, Paul stresses the value of the word gifts such as the utterance of wisdom and of understanding and of prophecy. To understand these elements in relation to that which we have been discussing, there are several points of importance. These gifts are clearly from one and the same Spirit. As we have come to understand them, the gifts of the Holy Spirit taking place in the body of Christ are actions of Jesus, the risen Lord in our midst, through the members of his body who are open and who have yielded to the inspirations of his Spirit. They are therefore extensions of the activity of the living Word of God in our midst, for such Jesus is. They are, therefore, in their operation, analogous to the proclamation of Scripture, although clearly they do not have the same value.

Later Types of Christian Assemblies

The identical pattern works itself out in the types of Christian assemblies which form the life of the Church from the New Testament generation down throughout history. Even within the New Testament period we see a pattern of assembly in which Christians continue to attend the Jewish synagogue in order to hear and respond to the Word of God, and then by themselves to celebrate their eucharistic meal in the presence of God's Word where their thanksgiving is complete.

Toward the end of this period it became clear that the Christians were permanently separated from the Jewish synagogues because their word and witness were increasingly unacceptable to the Jews. As they grew in numbers they began to hold their assemblies completely apart from the synagogues, bringing the synagogue pattern of worship to their eucharistic celebrations. In this way, before the celebration of the eucharist, they had the service of the Word. This is a response to and praise of God in and through his living Word proclaimed in the midst of his people. Thus the liturgy of the Word and the liturgy of the eucharist have been joined together in one assembly almost from the very beginnings of Christianity.

Third, we have evidence that the Christian people in the first 400 years of our era were accustomed to praying in their homes by themselves or perhaps in domestic groups, in small family meetings, at morning and evening, with their prayers adapted to the needs of those occasions. Furthermore we find evidence in the 3rd century that the Christian people were encouraged to pray also at the third, the sixth and the ninth hours of the day—that is to say at nine A.M., at noon, and at three P.M., in addition to their morning and evening prayers. This domestic pattern of prayer, which went on separately from the assembly of the whole people in a town or city, was the prevailing custom until the 4th century. Although the evidence is not altogether clear, we can discern a pattern of private assembly within the home. This assembly is not the whole Church, but members of the body, members of the Church, who continue to assemble whenever it is possible to hear and respond to the Word of God.

In the early 4th century, we find three major streams of developing piety which bring very clearly into the forefront a variety of Christian assemblies of the Word. First, two daily assemblies were held in the churches themselves, meant for all the people, at dawn and again at lamplighting at evening. These assemblies had heavy emphasis on the reading of and meditation upon Scripture as well as the use of appropriate psalms for the response of the people. This pattern existed in many churches, particularly in Palestine and Syria. It was, in fact, the daily prayer of the Church. The second strain was quite contemporary with the first and may be referred to under the classification of Egyptian monasticism. As Egyptian monasticism matured from its primitive beginnings, it developed a pattern of community assemblies for the monks; they would meet two or three times a day for Scripture reading, but with a very heavy emphasis on the reading and praying of the psalms as a perfect prayer and vehicle for meditation on the good things of God.

Third, we find a type of monasticism somewhat different in origin than the Egyptian, springing up in Palestine and in Syria around and in conjunction with the churches which were already conducting the two official daily assemblies. This type of monasticism was not carried on by monks but rather by free-lance ascetics, both

men and women. They came together on their own initiative in the church building, before and perhaps after
the regular ecclesiastical assemblies and at different intervals during the day. This Palestinian type of monasticism
yielded many different assemblies during the day and
night for hearing and responding to the Word of God,
for praising God with psalms and hymns.

From the eventual cross-influencing and fusing of different elements from these major patterns, a central pattern emerged throughout the whole Church, with minor
variations here and there, by the 5th and 6th centuries.
As the pattern formed, it firmed up that part of the worship of the Church which we refer to as the Divine Office
—the establishment of different times during the day
when it was possible for the Christian people, or at least
for some of them, to assemble together around the Word
of God. Eventually eight hours of prayer were established,
one in the middle of the night, another at dawn, then
short hours of prayer at the first, third, sixth and ninth
hours, then again at evening time, and finally at night
before retiring. Therefore, in addition to the great Sunday and festal celebrations of the eucharist which were
for the whole people of God, there was established at the
very beginning of the Middle Ages the pattern of meeting for prayer many times during the day and week.

Unfortunately the monastic influence on the ecclesial
assemblies for prayer was so heavy that this office became
more and more a clerical preserve and less and less an
assembly of the whole people. However, throughout the
Middle Ages a number of attempts were made to integrate the prayer life of the Christian people with these
types of official prayer meetings. In almost every medieval
town of any size one could find a choir of monks or canons
in the local church who would spend a good part of their
day singing the office. For a variety of reasons the people
themselves were unable to take part. However, several at-

tempts were made to enable the people at least to participate in the spirit of this prayer. The Angelus prayer for example, which was rung out at the times when the monks or canons were singing a particular hour of the office, was meant as a way for the people at home or at work in shop or fields to join themselves with the prayers going on in the church. In the later Middle Ages, there was a whole proliferation of little offices or prayer books for lay people which followed generally the same pattern as the Divine Office itself. Finally, the rosary may be seen as an attempt to give the people simple prayers they could remember and basic themes on which to meditate as they prayed throughout the day.

What we can see from all of this is that the whole Catholic tradition from its very early stages down to the present is characterized, as the Old Testament period was characterized, by assemblies, by meetings of God's people in a local place to hear the Word of God and to respond to God's Word, to respond to Christ, and, through that living Word, to enter more deeply into life with the Father.

It is quite true that the churches of the Reformation renewed the pastoral use of assemblies for preaching and prayer. This occurred in the area of official church order as well as on the more personal, unofficial level. A new form of the Divine Office arose, taking the shape of Bible reading in the home, and a variety of voluntary assemblies, such as those practiced by 16th-century Friends or the later Methodists, became common on the popular level. Clearly the ancestors of our separated brethren were not creating a new form of worship foreign to Catholicism, but rather were reviving a practice deeply rooted in Catholic tradition. While as Catholics we might disagree with some of the content of such meetings in recent centuries, we would not regard the structure of the assembly as something inimical to Catholicism.

Prayer Meetings Today

The Catholic liturgical revival of the 20th century and its companion, the Scripture movement, have paved the way for the prayer meetings we now experience in a thoroughly Catholic context. In the past seventy years, the introduction of popular participation in hymnody, the layman's missal, the praying of the Divine Office in the vernacular by religious and lay people, and the emergence of Bible vigils and services in churches and homes have revived our sense for the authentic tradition of a variety of assemblies of Word and praise. Vatican Council II gave its hearty endorsement to these developments.

The prayer meetings we experience today are an integral and authentic development of this pattern. In the prayer meeting we first assemble around God's living Word, conscious that Christ himself is in our midst. Second, in the prayer meeting as it is being experienced in the charismatic renewal in the Church today, nothing is more central than the sharing, reading, and proclamation of the written Word of God in the Bible. Third, the prayer meeting is characterized by the extended response to the Word of God in prayers of praise and thanksgiving which are so totally characteristic of the entire movement. Finally, in the prayer meeting we experience the exercise of the various ministry gifts, particularly the word gifts which we have already spoken of as an extension of the activity of the Word.

Thus the prayer meeting is authentic to the whole pattern of the Judaeo-Christian tradition. This is the very same pattern of God's Word coming among his people, speaking to and informing his people, leading them into deeper life. This very same pattern we see going as far back as God's revelation of himself to Abraham and the formation of his people in the old covenant; to the formation of the new people, the new covenant in the paschal mystery of Christ and the whole living out of that in the prayer meeting pattern of the Catholic Christian tradition. This is all part of our tradition and it finds a very contemporary expression in the prayer meetings we experience.

The prayer meeting therefore cannot possibly be spoken of as a Protestantizing activity; it is thoroughly rooted in the core of the Catholic worshiping tradition. It might be suggested here, at a time when the Divine Office is being examined with an eye toward its revivification in the Church, that the experience of the prayer meeting, which is cut out of the same cloth as the Divine Office originally was, may offer some answers for its renewal.

Some final considerations: The prayer meeting, because of its character as an assembly of praise and thanksgiving, has a basically eucharistic nature, for the word "eucharist" means basically praise and thanksgiving. This raises two possibilities for consideration. First, is it possible or desirable to conclude the prayer meeting with the banquet of our Lord's death and resurrection? A culminating eucharistic celebration may fit very well with a prayer meeting, while the prayer meeting may be seen as a form of the liturgy of the Word.

On the other side of the coin, might not some of the elements of the prayer meeting—particularly the dynamic proclamation of Scripture and the use of the word gifts —be integrated with the Word service of our Masses? As developments in liturgical practice begin to allow for more spontaneity in the assembly, it may be possible to move in this direction.

However, the history we have examined shows us that not every eucharistic assembly, not every meeting of praise and thanksgiving, is a Mass. There are many types of meetings for prayer in the Church—for example, the hours of the Divine Office which culminate in prayers of praise. This is an end in itself, and it should not be felt to be incomplete because it does not contain within itself the celebration of the sacrifice of the Mass.

The assembly of Christians led by the Spirit, the prayer meeting, is not just another meeting. It is unique. For as we gather together in the prayer meeting, it is the Word of God, Jesus himself, who by the power of the Holy Spirit lives in our midst. And as we gather, one in the Spirit, bound to each other and made one in Christ by that powerful Holy Spirit, we are truly unique, we are a manifestation of the body of Christ, we are an incarnation in space and time of the whole reality of the death and resurrection of Christ which is the life of the world. The prayer meeting is a place where God speaks to his people. It is an event where the Word of God pierces our hearts and enables us to be drawn more and more deeply into the personality of Jesus.

Dynamics of the Prayer Meeting

James Cavnar

We have come to see that it is for worship that the Lord has led us together in prayer meetings. The Lord draws us together in order that we might worship him as a people. St. Paul says in the epistle to the Ephesians that "we have been appointed to live for the praise of his glory" (Eph. 1, 12). The prayer meeting is primarily our coming together to praise the Lord, to adore him, to manifest his glory, and to share those things that bring out his glory. Worship means that our prayer meetings must turn to God. We are not gathered simply to share our insights but to look to God and worship him.

The second purpose of prayer meetings flows out of the first—to form the body of Christ, to draw us together in love of one another that we might become the body of Christ.

Worship in the Prayer Meeting

If our prayer meetings are to be truly worshipful they must first of all be explicitly centered on God. The focus of the prayer meeting is God himself. The prayer meeting will be more worship-filled if the leader calls people to this kind of prayer at the beginning of the meeting. I remember when we visited a city that was beginning to have prayer meetings but where there was little spirit of praise.

The prayer meeting was mostly made up of discussion and praying for various petitions. The people said to me, "Jim, the people here aren't ready for the kind of worship you have in your prayer meetings." So when we gathered for the prayer meeting—and there were many new people there, too—I got up and spoke. I called everyone to worship and explained how we can worship together. We began with a worshipful song and started to praise the Lord aloud. And it was truly amazing to see how people began to give themselves to praise of God, and then the spiritual gifts began to work in a way that the group had never experienced before. And it came because we began by praising the Lord. I could see that it was the explicit exhortation to worship that focused people upon the Lord.

Choruses or songs that are easily memorized are especially helpful, since they can be started without introduction as a prayer. Sometimes the worship in a prayer meeting might consist of a series of songs started one after another by different people. Lively songs, quiet songs, psalms, hymns—all have a place in the worship of the prayer meeting. Worship is encouraged by the use of joyous and prayerful songs. Many choruses and songs we sing are songs of praise and adoration. They create an atmosphere of worship and give the whole community a way to express praise together.

Bringing out the glory of God is a third thing that leads people to worship. Through testimony and sharing, people tell of events in their life that bring out the power and glory of God. Recently at a prayer meeting a visiting priest stood to tell what the Lord had been doing in his area. He described several remarkable healings; he related the story of a dramatic conversion; he told of the Lord's providential leading in providing a house for a community center. When he concluded, all the people with one voice began to praise God enthusiastically because we were so overwhelmed at seeing the glory of God as revealed in his story, ". . . singing aloud a song of thanksgiving, and telling all thy wondrous deeds."

A fourth way of bringing us to worship more is "waiting upon the Lord." Our prayer meetings will never be worshipful or edifying if they are only the work of man. Rather, as Jesus said to the woman at the well in Samaria, "The true worshipers will worship in spirit and truth, for such the Father seeks to worship him" (Jn. 4, 23). We can worship in the Spirit only if we are in contact with God because it is God's Spirit that must lead us to worship. This means "waiting upon the Lord"—perhaps waiting in silence, waiting for the Holy Spirit to move us, and looking for the Holy Spirit's action among us. The Holy Spirit can speak through prophecy and bring us to praise and worship when no amount of effort to push us in that direction would have worked. Occasionally a person may be moved to stand and speak an inspired word. I remember a fellow who got up in one of our prayer meetings and simply said to us, "I sense that the Lord's gift to us tonight is one of peace." And even as he spoke the Holy Spirit brought a spirit of peace to the whole community, and from that moment on there was a peaceful and restful spirit of praise throughout the meeting. Singing in the Spirit is a way too that the Holy Spirit can move to cause us to worship. A few may begin to sing in the Spirit, using the gift of tongues, and others are led to yield to praise and to sing also.

The first and most important reason for our prayer meetings is the worship of God, and this means that it is the Holy Spirit who must empower our meetings. It is impossible to worship in the Spirit by doing it mechanically. Let us pray earnestly in each prayer meeting that the Holy Spirit will move us to the praise of God.

Building the Body of Christ

The second reason for prayer meetings is to form the body of Christ. Remember the law of the Lord Jesus, "This is the new commandment that I give you, that you love one another as I have loved you" (Jn. 13, 34). The love of the brethren is the law of the Lord. So as we gather in a prayer meeting we should greet one another with affection and with brotherly love, expressed in handshakes and embraces and greetings. And during the prayer meeting we should desire to help one another. How many fail to share or to prophesy out of fear, wondering, "What will people think of me?" Shouldn't we first ask: "Is this something that will help my brother?" For if I love my brothers, won't I want to do anything that the Holy Spirit gives me that I know will help them and build them up?

A spirit of humility and gentleness should mark our contributions to the prayer meeting, not forcing ourselves or our testimony upon the meeting but simply offering ourselves in a humble way to be used by the Lord for the building up of our brothers. It is important that everyone at the prayer meeting is participating, seeking the Lord and listening to the Holy Spirit. There will be times when the Lord draws us to speak and times when he moves us to silence in awe-filled adoration. At such moments someone who hastily and abruptly speaks out can interrupt the flow of the Holy Spirit during that meeting. We must all be in prayer and sensitive to the Spirit. We can help one another to learn to do this. People frequently come up after a meeting and ask what we thought about what they said. This gives us the opportunity to give them some "feedback" so they can see whether or not their participation was effective. Leaders, too, should have someone comment on their contributions.

The Holy Spirit also works through the spiritual gifts to build the body of Christ. St. Paul says that "he who prophesies speaks to men for their upbuilding and encouragement and consolation" (1 Cor. 14, 3). Prophecy in a prayer meeting plays the same role as every other contribution—it builds and forms the body of Christ. The most important test of prophecy is this: Does it build the body of Christ? Supernatural manifestations have no value in themselves in the Christian life, but they do have value if they build up the community. Therefore the way that a spiritual gift is manifested is important. A prophecy should be given in such a way that it is edifying. Sometimes prophecy can be given so violently that it is frightening, or so timidly that it is indistinct.

Teaching also builds the body of Christ, and the lack of good teaching is the greatest weakness in most prayer groups. When a prayer group is just beginning, teaching is needed if there is even going to be prayer—teaching about what the gifts of the Spirit are, how they are exercised, and the proper attitudes we need toward them. Teaching from the leaders of a group also provides some recognized and sound instruction that people can rely on. In an open prayer meeting where all are free to speak, there are bound to be some things said that are of questionable reliability. Teaching from someone who is recognized and accepted provides a sound norm for the group and gives new people some reliable instruction. Many who come for the first time to a prayer meeting have no way of distinguishing what is good or bad in the prayer meeting and are likely to accept as normative something said by one person in the group when the rest of the group would have treated it with greater circumspection.

There are many forms that teaching can take in the prayer meeting. A spontaneous teaching inspired by the Holy Spirit at the prayer meeting is only one way. The "teacher" can seek the Lord in advance and pray for the Holy Spirit to guide him as he prepares a talk for the prayer meetings. Many times the Lord will lead the whole prayer meeting along the same theme as the prepared teaching. I can recall one time when a man who came prepared to speak on the topic of faith was surprised to find that, by the time he was called on, virtually his whole message had already been given in prophecy and sharing and people had already read almost every Scripture passage he had intended to refer to. His teaching provided a perfect summary of the Lord's Word to that meeting.

To worship together as the Lord's people, to build and to form one another as the body of Christ—this is the purpose of prayer meetings, whether by "prayer meetings" we mean a group of 10 or a group of 500 persons.

Types of Prayer Meetings

There are different types of prayer meetings that entail different types of leadership and service, that involve different types of person relationships, and that fulfill different functions.

The first type is what we'll call a prayer group—a small group, perhaps 10 to 20 persons, that may meet in a home. The leadership of such a prayer group may be very indefinite, or perhaps the leader might be the host in whose home the meeting is held. Or there might be a rotating leadership with different ones taking turns.

If there are many new people at a prayer meeting, it will, of course, change the tone of the prayer meeting, particularly when the group is relatively small to begin with. When we have a prayer group that has been meeting every week and suddenly half the people there one night are new, the other half of us must be much more attentive to the Spirit in setting the tone and giving leadership, calling forth faith, prayer, and various other things. If one person is the leader, he'll have to be much more attentive to the Spirit. When half the people are new to the prayer meeting, it can very easily become dead because they won't know how to participate, and others, perhaps not aware of the special burden which the Holy Spirit is giving them to lead people, may fail to respond to the Spirit if they are not conscious of the need.

The service offered by a small prayer group is almost necessarily partial. There simply are not enough people to provide much teaching or preparation for new people or much formation for the prayer group. However, the small prayer group can have a variety of functions. It might be the first prayer group in a city and form the first step toward the formation of a larger prayer meeting. Or perhaps after the growth of a larger prayer meeting there may be smaller prayer groups for more personal fellowship within the larger prayer community. Or it may simply be the Lord's plan for a group of people as they follow him that they remain a small prayer group for a time.

The personal relationships found in a prayer group are relationships of personal friendship. It is possible for people to know everyone quite well and intimately. During the prayer meeting they can share personal and even intimate things since they are among close friends. Frequently, as a prayer group begins to grow and reaches the size of thirty or forty persons, we hear people say, "Oh, but we just don't seem to have that close friendship and unity we used to have. Maybe we should break up into several small groups." The discontent thus expressed is usually a growing pain that accompanies the transition from being a prayer group to becoming a larger "prayer meeting." Rather than fragmenting, it would be better to form smaller groups within the community and maintain the larger prayer meeting for all. In the larger prayer meeting there is a greater witness to visitors, a greater opportunity for gifts and services to mature, and a greater support for the individual Christian and for smaller prayer groups. Most small prayer groups seem to lack the internal resources to persevere very fruitfully if they are isolated.

A second type of prayer meeting is what I'll simply refer to as a "prayer meeting." This would be a larger group. As a small prayer group begins to grow and becomes larger than about thirty persons, many changes occur. There begin to be more new people, a greater demand for service to them, and a greater need for recognized leadership. There is also a fuller manifestation of the gifts of the Spirit. And the prayer meeting operates in a different way than a prayer group. In a prayer meeting you might regularly have as many as 400 or 500 people. (There are now many prayer meetings of this size in various cities around the country.) The leadership required in a prayer meeting is that of a pastoral team. This requires a stable group of leaders who probably meet together at another time to take care of the various services needed in the prayer meeting itself. There will probably be one (or possibly two or three) who will regularly lead the prayer meeting to provide stability and continuity. It is much easier for a community spirit and unity in worship to develop if the style of leadership in the prayer meeting is familiar from week to week and people learn how to respond to the leader.

The services in a prayer meeting should be more developed than in a smaller group. There will probably be an explanation session for new people. There will be a more developed preparation for introducing people to the life in the Spirit and praying with them for the baptism of the Spirit. As new people are introduced to the baptism of the Spirit, they can receive more teaching about growth, walking in the Spirit, spiritual gifts, and the importance of Christian community.

Another element in the service of the prayer meet-

ing is teaching. Many prayer meetings regularly receive
prepared teaching from some of the leaders who have
that ministry. There may also be classes or workshops before or after the prayer meeting to provide a service of
teaching and spiritual formation.

A prayer meeting has the possibility of experiencing
a great variety of ministries. Within a prayer meeting one
should begin to see the development of people with the
ministry of prophecy—not only prophesying but finding
gifts of prophecy and revelation working in their lives in
a regular way for the upbuilding of the community.
Teachers begin to become aware of their ministry and exercise it regularly in the prayer community. There may
be ministries of service or of exhorting that begin to
mature and can be exercised regularly in the community.

The type of human relationship that characterizes a
prayer meeting is what we might call a "community-type"
personal relationship. We know and love one another as
brothers in Christ, and we share a very deep commitment and unity in the Spirit, though we may not know
each person in an intimate way. This type of personal relationship involves a commitment to one another to be a
community. As we read in the epistle to the Hebrews:
"Let us consider how to stir up one another to love and
good works, not neglecting to meet together, as is the
habit of some, but encouraging one another, and all the
more as you see the Day drawing near" (10:24–26). In a
prayer meeting there is a need for people to be consciously aware that they must not "neglect to meet together" if they are to grow into a real community. As
members of such a prayer meeting we must make the decision to maintain unity and love even though there may
not be, especially at the beginning, deep bonds of personal friendship with everyone.

A prayer meeting functions as the assembly of a community of Christians who are sharing their lives and helping one another to live in the Spirit of Jesus. And at the

prayer meeting there is a building up of the body of Christ and the witness of the community to the world.

Flowing in the Spirit

A prayer meeting should flow naturally in the Spirit. If worship is truly the heart of the prayer meeting, then worship will happen more readily. We begin a prayer meeting with a period of worship, singing choruses and worshipful songs, praying all together in a "word of prayer" (where each of us praises the Lord in his own words aloud in a way that makes the spirit of prayer visible throughout the entire community). This is one of the best forms of prayer for building a community of prayer. During this period the Holy Spirit may move us to sing in the Spirit. Individual people will pray aloud. Members of the community may give exhortations to worship or to turn to the Lord as the Spirit moves them. During this time of praise, the spiritual gifts, such as prophecy, and tongues with interpretation, will be manifested. The prayer meeting flows naturally with prayers of praise continually rising throughout the meeting. Because the prayer meeting begins with a period of worship, the sharing and prophecy flow out of a unified spirit of praise and work to build or enhance that spirit. The people should maintain an attitude of prayer and reverence, actively seeking to glorify God and edify the body of Christ. And so when a person stands to share or teach, it does not interrupt the spirit of worship but should build that spirit.

Everyone in the prayer meeting should be actively looking to the Lord and praying—listening to the Lord and listening in the Spirit to the things said in the prayer meeting. Jesus truly is Lord of the meeting and he will bring good out of all that takes place. So we listen "in the Spirit," asking, "What is it that the Lord is saying here?" And we must also be sensitive to the Spirit before we speak, asking: "O Holy Spirit, is this what you would desire me to share?" And asking too: "Is this the right time, or should I wait?"

Many prayer meetings struggle constantly with dead-ness. We can meet this problem by exhorting people to worship the Lord actively in singing and especially in the "word of prayer." We can also encourage people to express their prayer aloud, no matter how inadequate they think it. We can encourage all to come prepared by praying before the meeting and asking the Lord what he would like them to share or sing, etc. There should be a spirit of freedom, a lively praise and worship where people feel free to praise the Lord aloud, to sing in the Spirit, to stand, or even to raise their hands. This type of freedom grows in a prayer meeting if there is an atmos-phere of love and encouragement, so that each has the sense of being supported in his efforts by his brothers and is willing to share and pray and manifest the spiritual gifts despite the fear of mistakes. We can at least learn from mistakes, but deadness and non-participation stifle the Spirit.

Order in the Prayer Meeting

A good prayer meeting has a sense of order in it. As St. Paul says, "Our God is not a God of confusion, but of peace." There will be good order if there is good leadership and if people are sensitive to that leadership. It is the responsibility of the leader to introduce the prayer meeting by explaining whatever needs to be said about worship and the spiritual gifts. The leader should maintain good order. If there is a message in tongues and before it is interpreted someone speaks, then he should stand and say, "Let us wait for the interpretation." There should be a spirit of peace in the prayer meeting, not of haste or anxiety or fear.

One practical thing that helps is having a definite length of time for the meeting. An hour and a half to two hours is a good length. In a home prayer group it may be possible to pray as long as everyone wants and go on for four or five hours. But in a large prayer meeting people will not come regularly if they never know when they will be able to get home to bed. The length of a prayer meeting should not be overly tiring or deadening.

A prayer meeting can have structure. In fact it needs some structure if a large group of people are to worship together in peace and with order. Many successful prayer meetings—though not having a rigid structure—tend to follow this pattern: The meeting begins with singing; then there is a short talk from the leader explaining the prayer meeting, welcoming new people, and exhorting people to worship. There follows a period of praise and worship, singing choruses and songs, perhaps with words of exhortation, readings from Scripture, and prophecy in the midst of a continual flow of worship and praise. This might continue for a half hour or even an hour. Then there is more sharing as people tell what the Lord has done in their lives, or explain some insight the Lord has given them. In addition to these spontaneous contributions, the leader might call on someone who has come prepared to tell the story of his own conversion or "baptism in the Spirit." Many groups regularly have a short teaching by one of the leaders. There is prayer throughout, with singing or periods of quiet meditation upon the words of the Lord. Everything comes to a close with announcements and lively songs of praise to God. Before or after the meeting there should be an introductory session for newcomers, and there may also be separate meetings for persons who wish a fuller life in the Spirit. Special rooms may be designated for these sessions.

Any pattern for a prayer meeting can become deadening if followed too rigidly, but it does help the growth of a meeting when such patterns are instruments of the Lord.

In a prayer meeting, unlike the situation in a prayer group, it is usually impossible to pray for the individual intentions of all those who want to ask. There are simply too many. It is spiritually difficult, too, because it is hard to pray in faith for so many intentions when there is no time to discuss how to pray or to hear the details of the need which would enable us to pray with greater sincerity. In such cases, prayers for special intentions can become mechanical. Lumping many intentions together for a general prayer is even more impersonal and mechanical. Many prayer meetings now have a special meeting afterward where those desiring prayer for personal needs can be prayed with, and where personal intentions can be brought for concerted group prayer. Prophetic and teaching gifts can be exercised fully here as each person is prayed for.

Spiritual Gifts and Music

The gifts of the Holy Spirit should certainly flow freely during a prayer meeting. If a prayer meeting is truly centered upon the Lord and if there is a genuine seeking of God in worship, this will greatly prepare us to receive the spiritual gifts. Many problems with spiritual gifts are avoided when the gifts flow out of a spirit of worshipful prayer. In a new prayer group, not experienced in the spiritual gifts, it helps to have some kind of teaching and discussion about the gifts. The leaders should exhort the group to pray together for the spiritual gifts so that all are of one heart and mind in desiring and seeking the gifts of the Spirit.

It is essential in a prayer meeting to "give God a

chance." If we get so busy talking about our ideas and problems that we never stop to listen to the Lord in quietness, chances are the Lord will have difficulty getting a word in edgewise. This is especially true in a group just growing in the spiritual gifts, since people need time to respond to the Spirit and overcome their fears of stepping out to give their first prophecy. But a group needs to give *itself* a chance too. People must be willing to make mistakes and must try to yield to the Spirit who desires to make his gifts manifest among them.

The ministry of music is another important service in a prayer meeting. We use the term *ministry* of music because there is a lot more involved than just having people who can play the guitar and lead songs. There is a need to give some care to the selection of songs that are edifying, that are centered on the Lord and that lead people to prayer. Singing in a prayer meeting is not like singing at a hootenanny; it is a form of prayer. Music can set a tone of reverence and worship. It can bring forth exuberance and joy. It can set the direction of the meeting for good or ill. During a prayer meeting it is good to have freedom so that anyone can start a song and all can join it. Yet it is also good to have someone who can provide a continuous formation of the community in music to prepare songs that are edifying and to lead the group in song.

Everyone in a prayer meeting is an active participant, though he may not prophesy or speak to the group at all. Each should be actively looking to the Lord Jesus, not letting his mind wander from topic to topic but reminding himself of the presence of our Lord. Each should be listening carefully to all that is said, weighing all things, asking, "Lord, what are you saying to me through all these things?" Each should actively desire to contribute as the Holy Spirit directs. And, finally, each should pray earnestly, whether silently or aloud. If there is not full participation in the prayer meeting by everyone, the work of God's Spirit is hindered or quenched. The presence of many who are not participating spiritually in the meeting is like dead weight. But where there is full participation, even silence is alive with the Spirit.

Prayer meetings have to be prepared for; this is one way that everyone can participate. The first and most important way of preparation is through the individual prayer of all participants. If a prayer meeting becomes dead and lifeless, very often it's because the people do not have a deepening personal contact with God. Growth in private prayer is essential for the growth of a community in a prayer meeting. What happens in the prayer meeting is that this personal life of prayer surfaces in the whole community.

Another important way of preparation is to pray specifically for the meeting and for the leaders of the meeting. One should also come having prayed that he himself might be open to the Spirit during the meeting. One should come prepared to receive whatever God wants him to receive. He should come with a heart prepared to welcome the Lord and with a mind open to receiving what the Lord says. Even more, one should come with something to give. We can ask the Lord beforehand, "What should I do tonight? What will you give me to share with my brothers and sisters?" We should come to prayer meetings in a spirit of charity, self-sacrificing charity that seeks above all the love of one's brothers, and above all to give to one another and strengthen one another.

Starting a Prayer Meeting

It is the Lord who draws together a prayer meeting; no amount of work by us alone can bring forth the fruit which the work of the Spirit produces. As a small group gathers in a home and begins to pray together, they need to entrust all things to the Lord, offering themselves in a humble way to the Lord who alone can work great wonders. But our little experience suggests some practical guidelines:

1. Let the prayer meeting be explicitly "pentecostal" from the very beginning so that all persons are aware that we are here to seek the gifts of the Spirit and desire his full working among us. It is sometimes impossible to move a whole group together to Spirit-filled worship and prayer if they have first grown accustomed to a non-charismatic form of prayer meeting.

2. Remember that a prayer meeting is not a discussion. Sometimes during a meeting we may have something very like a discussion as a theme develops. One person may make a statement on a particular theme, and it may bring to another person's mind something that the Spirit may move him to say. And there may be a prophecy that will reinforce the theme. We may see a theme building up with different people contributing to it. But this is very different from a discussion. There's a place in the Christian life for discussions—a very important one—but usually not in the prayer meeting where it can completely disrupt the unity in the Spirit and the spirit of prayer in the meeting.

3. Move quickly to establishment of separate instruction and prayer for new people so that the prayer meeting does not spend its time discussing the basic things week after week. At the beginning of the prayer meeting a little announcement can be made, informing new people that there will be time after the meeting for discussion of the baptism of the Spirit. In this way the prayer meeting can grow in a spirit of worship from week to week and not be constantly repetitious.

4. Don't seek publicity. Let the Holy Spirit bring people, so that the prayer meeting can grow naturally and organically. When a prayer meeting grows too

rapidly, the new people often dominate and set the tone of the meeting, when the tone and direction should be set by the members of the prayer group. Publicity can also entangle a group in needless controversy and criticism and interfere with its growth.

5. It is important not to allow classical pentecostals to dominate the meeting. Most Catholics are simply unprepared for the style of prayer or theology of classical pentecostals (who frequently are men and women of great experience and strong leadership ability) who, in an attempt to help, unconsciously direct the prayer meeting into a style unedifying to most Catholics. The problem is mainly cultural, but it is nonetheless a problem. It may be necessary for the leaders to talk with them privately and explain the difficulty if a problem arises.

6. We must learn how to help "problem people"— those with psychological and spiritual problems that emerge as obstacles in the prayer meeting. Their sharings may be confusing or even frightening. They may tend to dominate without edifying. Love for them requires that we help them. Love for the brethren requires that we prevent their putting obstacles in the way of other sincere people. The awareness of a problem should be brought to the attention of leaders who should take the responsibility of talking with the person, explaining the reactions of others and discussing with them the problems they are struggling with. It may be advisable to ask them not to manifest spiritual gifts or speak very much in the meeting until some of the problems have been worked out. Those with serious disturbances should be asked not to speak at all for a time. Such a person needs to give his attention to receiving help for the healing of his mind; he is in no position to minister to others. Let us take on the responsibility to care for such people in every way we can, knowing that God desires their wholeness and happiness.

7. Don't focus on the devil. Confrontations with

Satan will arise, and they can be dealt with as they do, but one of the greatest mistakes is beginning to focus on Satan too much—demon-hunting. Focus instead on worship and on the love of God; when conflicts with the devil must be dealt with directly, the Lord will show the way. An over-concern for the devil can undermine a prayer group.

A prayer meeting is not an isolated event for the Christian. It should be the expression of a community of Christians whose life is shared throughout the week in other ways, too. The life of the community is focused at the prayer meeting and built up there, yet there is more to that life than just the prayer meeting. The prayer meeting is a part of the full life we seek as the Holy Spirit forms us day by day into the body of Christ.

Baptism in the Holy Spirit and Christian Spirituality

Dorothy Ranaghan

In the glory and the joy of those first few days, weeks, and months that followed our experience of charismatic renewal, our baptism into the Spirit of God, a universal characteristic that we all experienced was a desire and a new ability to praise God, to respond with all of our being to the overflowing love that he has for us. Our joy and exultation in the very real awareness of his presence was matched by an ability to respond and an ability to pray that many of us found exciting, refreshing, yet puzzling, because everyone realized that the work begun within us was essentially and utterly a gift.

In the life of faith everything is a gift. All life, all hope, all holiness comes from God. How do we respond to the gift of God? How do we respond to the gifts of the Holy Spirit? If we see in this charismatic renewal a new beginning for each of us and for the whole Church, then the image in Scripture of the seed that falls to the ground should stir us to allow this new life to grow and develop within us as in good and fertile soil. It should lead us to take advantage of the grace period which surrounds our baptism in the Spirit, and to truly begin to walk in the Spirit. Experience has shown that there is a new desire to pray, a new desire to read Scripture, a new desire to begin to form a life of deep spiritual growth. It is up to us, then, to take advantage of that new desire and new ability and, with the grace of God, to make an opening, a place in our lives for the beginnings of deep growth, growth that is solid and strong, with roots in the whole tradition of the Christian experience.

More and more we have come to see that to be baptized into the Holy Spirit is an important element in the full Christian life which our Lord intended each of us to live. But it is not an isolated experience. The baptism in the Holy Spirit is intimately related to the whole Christian life. Though its reception will transform one's relationship with God and men, it is not a synonym for the Christian life. It is an empowering that enables us to live that life, but its reception does not circumvent the normal economy of God's plan.

A Way for Everyday Life

The experience of the baptism in the Holy Spirit is not meant to be only a peak, a high, a transformation, a pink cloud, beautiful but remembered only as a past event. It is meant to be the experienced heartbeat of a daily walk with the Lord, a foundation stone on which to lay one foot after another as we step and walk in the Spirit. The plan of God for men is not just that we come to know him, nor even just that we become filled with his Spirit. Because, as with the very first Pentecost in the life of the Church, this is only the beginning. God wills to draw us all into a deep relationship of love with himself. He wants nothing less than that we become holy as he is holy, that we become one with him. The plan and the prayer of Jesus is: "Father, may they be one in us, as you are in me and I am in you" (Jn. 17, 21).

Our question then becomes one of seeing what channels exist which will allow the baptism in the Holy Spirit to flow through our lives. What channels are open to us that will facilitate a real growth in a disciplined life of prayer and a deepened relationship of love with the three Persons who have called us to share their life and love?

This is the aim of Christian spirituality. It is a plan, a means, an attempt to find a way of living every day in a growing union with God. It is a way by which we can begin to integrate, assimilate, and encompass the reality of Jesus Christ into our daily existence. It is a way of response to the call to holiness.

To be sure, there are some Christians who really don't want to grow in the life of the Spirit. They are bored by the many dimensions of Christian spirituality. Among the more "liberal" people in our Church today, the whole concept of growth in the spiritual life and prayer is suspect. Having finally realized the truth of our need to love our fellow men (a truth to which each Christian must add the Amen of his deeds), they tend to identify prayer with action. The critical flaw, however, is that while Jesus is truly seen to be in the "other," both the possibility and the experience of the presence of the risen Lord himself are denied.

On the other end of the faith spectrum, even after the baptism in the Spirit, there have been those who shun or ignore the demands of growth. Some people want to cling only to their charismatic experience. Anyone who has felt the personal touch of Jesus burning deep and tender within his heart—in the here, in the now, where I am and where I live—that person has known real love. It is in this vital experience of love in a personal meeting with the Lord Jesus that the spiritual life begins. But we must learn, too, that to nurture that experience alone, as beautiful as it is, as consoling as it is, is not enough. Is there any marriage or any love relationship which nourishes only one peak experience—a wedding day, for instance? We all know that would be foolish. Husband

and wife in living life together can never forget the common sharing of their first days together. If you didn't think of the first days when you met and fell in love, that would be abnormal. Growth must come through that first meeting, through those first days of falling in love, through the honeymoon into the new and exciting and deeper realms of shared tasks and goals, of birth and childhood—all the common joys and trials, burdens, tears, and laughter that make up the whole of life.

This, too, is the essential message of Christianity. We have died and have risen with Christ, not for a new experience, but to live a life, and life demands growth. And so we have to get on with it. Some people say: "Oh, I don't want to study the history of the Church, I don't want to study Scripture, I don't want to find out about prayer, or read or learn or be directed, or witness or become involved in the world." These are ways we grow in Christ, but they say, "I want only to sit with my Lord." A husband and wife just cannot live a whole life together in an unspoken acceptance of the gift of each other. If they ever stop trying to learn more about each other and how to please each other, or if they ever stop telling each other of their love, one day they may awaken to find that that love which they now want to celebrate has slipped away. The life of faith is a life of love, a life in which we are more and more being drawn into personal intimacy with a personal God.

How can we grow in union with God in the person of Jesus? First of all, it should be clear that no one ever becomes a person to us except through some form of communication, through dialogue. If I don't talk to you, I won't know very much about you. Today, this is a commonly accepted insight of psychology. From all eternity it has been essential in the plan of God. Christian revelation is essentially a Word. The Father has spoken his

Word to us—Jesus. Jesus contains within himself the full, inexhaustible richness of the message of God to man.

Jesus is a Word with and in whom we can speak. Prayer for the Christian is simply this. I can speak to the Lord God in Jesus and through the power of the Holy Spirit. In Jesus, united with him in his incarnation, my prayer is placed directly before the Father, and it is not an empty prayer but a prayer filled with the power of the Spirit.

And he speaks to me. When we are open, yielding and silent, the Word of God to our hearts is quite clear and direct and more real than the beating of our own heart. The Word of God is not, however, just confined to the interior witness of the Spirit to one inspired individual. Though we have all heard the voice of the Lord in this way, anxiety, aridity, doubt or trouble of any kind can seemingly close off this avenue of communication. The Word of God is not so limited. The Word of God is spoken forever, continually, a Word alive, a Word that gives life.

It is in the liturgical assembly, when the people of God meet together to hear this Word, that we find the wellspring of all authentic Christian spirituality. In the liturgy we find the full proclamation and participation in the total mystery of Christ. In the liturgy (eucharist, sacraments and Divine Office) we have the highest form of worship. Praise and thanksgiving are the very heart and core and center of the activity of Jesus in the liturgy of his body. The liturgy is an indispensable source of our Christian life.

In this chapter, therefore, we will not be concerned with inventing a new "pentecostal spirituality." Pentecostal spirituality as such does not exist any more than does a lay spirituality or a monastic spirituality, and yet how often we hear those terms. There are not many different spiritualities. We can emphasize some aspect or create a situational or historical adaptation (as was done in the rich medieval mystic tradition), but at root there is only one spirituality, and that lies in man's response to the Gospel of Jesus Christ as proclaimed by the Church.

A People of Praise

Many communities formed in the wake of the charismatic renewal that is sweeping through the Church have been led through the Scriptures and through prophecy to see that one of the many purposes of the Lord in this "outpouring" is to "raise up a people of praise," a people centered on praise and worship and thanksgiving. At our prayer meetings, one of the favorite hymns states: "Praise him in the morning, praise him in the noontime . . . praise him when the sun goes down." Our hope, our task, our commission is to center our day, week, month, year, to center our lives around the Word of God in prayer, praise, worship and thanksgiving.

The liturgical calendar gives focus and vision to this goal. It is like a seamless garment which gradually unfolds the total mystery of Jesus as contained in the Scriptures. It is meant to become the fabric of our lives. To become the body of Christ in this world, to become totally and wholly consecrated to the Lord, we must live his life, death and resurrection. To become one with him we must "put on the Lord Jesus Christ," we must live again through the liturgy the fullness of his life. Jesus is the same yesterday, today and tomorrow, and therefore we should not be brought into isolated units of his life, but become constantly centered on the total Christ. The only place in which this centrality, this wholeness, is maintained is in the liturgy.

Liturgy is essentially eucharist. The word "eucharist" means thanksgiving. All who are called to praise and thanksgiving are therefore called to be a eucharistic people. It is in the celebration of the Eucharist that the Christian people assemble to hear and respond to the Word of God most fully. For in the celebration of the Eucharist, the living Word of God, Jesus Christ, the risen Lord, is intensely and uniquely present in the midst of his body.

At the Last Supper, Jesus identified his life-giving death and resurrection—that is, his sacrifice which yields for us the gift of salvation—with this eucharistic meal, and he told us to continue its celebration so that it might continue to be the source of our participation in his life with the Father. Jesus clearly identified himself, himself-in-sacrifice, with the covenant foods of specially blessed bread and wine. Thus he told us that his death was the basis of the new and fulfilled covenant, the source of our salvation. In identifying the transformed sacrificial meal with his death on the cross, he assured us that his death was truly the sacrifice of the new law. In identifying his sacrificial death with the new covenant food and commanding us to continue its celebration, he gave us the rite of the new law by which the new memorial might be made, by which the reality of his death and resurrection might be recalled and made really present. Just as the Jews in the annual memorial celebration of the Passover renewed, through their participation in the meal, the covenant of the old law, so now the Christian people, in breaking this bread and sharing this cup, renew and re-affirm the new covenant in their midst. Therefore, the totality of the Christ-event, the wholeness of the paschal mystery, the whole meaning, the whole power, the whole force, the whole reality of the life, death, resurrection, ascension and sending of the Spirit, are all objectively present in the celebration of the eucharist. It is there that the Christian people meet the risen Lord most fully and most uniquely. It is there that the past events are made effectively present in the midst of the people, and the ongoing life in Christ and the Spirit flows from this event.

We are a eucharistic people. It is our purpose to be the body of Christ in a paschal attitude, continually celebrating the Christ-event. And while that takes place in all our lives, it happens most uniquely, most intensely, most effectively in our celebration of the eucharist. Therefore everything in Christian life seems to point to, or to flow from, the eucharistic celebration. All the sacraments either initiate us into the eucharistic assembly or sustain us in that eucharistic life, and from the eucharist the mission and apostolate of the Church flows. The life of Christ, that life in which we partake in the eucharistic celebration, is the source of all other Christian life.

Clearly, then, liturgy must not be thought of as merely the external worship of the Church (everything else being internal and therefore more real); it is not just external ritual, symbolic action—it is symbolic action that is worship. It is the worship of the Church. One reason that we feel the need to introduce people continually into the "liturgical" form of piety is that many people, filled with a new desire to pray and wanting a deepened spiritual life, go about it by picking and choosing at all little pieces of good things. A fragmented piety begins to splinter their lives. And they become over-extended. They want to pray, to go to Mass, to read Scripture, to say rosaries, to make novenas, the way of the cross and devotions of all kinds; they want to make visits to the Blessed Sacrament and to meditate. And all of these are good things. But a person's day and experience can appear like a patchwork quilt when he is finished, so that at the end of a day of trying to do good things and grow in prayer and follow the Lord, he may feel more exhausted from the sheer effort and confusion of sustaining and relating all his "practices" than the freedom and the joy of the Lord would suppose. It is not meant to be that way. It would be so easy to allow everything to flow from the eucharist, from the paschal mystery of Christ. When liturgical piety fills our lives, it centers our day on Jesus, centers our months, our years, and our seasons on Jesus. We become a eucharistic people, a "people of praise." Every Sunday we celebrate, through the eucharist, the presence of the risen Lord. Every Sunday is an Easter in miniature. We rejoice in the good news: "He has risen! Alleluia!"

Praying the Divine Office

In the Divine Office we find a practical means of embodying and extending this Sunday liturgy into daily life. The Divine Office, composed primarily of psalms and specially selected Scripture readings, carries into daily life the themes of the various eucharistic seasons. In the preface of *Morning Praise and Evensong,* the author says: "The Divine Office . . . remains an essential and integral part of the Church's worship. Together with the Mass and the sacraments it constitutes the great anthem of perpetual praise and petition which the whole Christ, head and members, presents at every moment to the heavenly Father."

The Office is the continual, disciplined sanctification of the seasons of the year and the "hours" of the day. The two main "hours" of the Office are meant to sanctify our morning and our evening. The Word of God should greet our morning, fill our days, and be the last thing we sing in the evening. During Morning Praise (or Lauds) our minds and our hearts are turned to praise of God in the universe, praise for being the Lord who has brought us to a new day. In Vespers, the "hinge" of nighttime, the people of God consider the past acts of God on their behalf. Psalms form the core of prayer and praise in the structure of the Office. And as we know, the psalms are unbeatable as a school of praise and thanksgiving, teaching us the merciful, glorious, faithful love of the living God.

The Divine Office is the way God's people can assemble to hear and respond to the living Word in their midst daily. In the Divine Office as it is structured throughout the seasons of the year (Advent to Pentecost), the people of God are enabled to commemorate, to recall and to reflect upon the many different phases in the totality of the mystery of Christ. The spacing of the readings and lessons from both the Old and New Testaments and the Fathers of the Church, as well as the apportionment of various parts of the Psalter to different times and seasons, enables us to dig deeply into the treasures of our Christian heritage.

Either alone, as families or as communities, with or without a priest, we can recite or sing the Divine Office. Prayer in this way acquires a certain depth, a level of the actualization of the wonderful works of God among his people in our own consciousness, and it enables us to go deeper into the mystery of salvation in and through the whole prayer of the Church.

All of this provides a fertile field for meditation. Reminded of the goodness of the Lord, of his saving love toward us, we are drawn to respond. There should be time every day of our lives to respond in love, to deepen our relationship with Jesus. We should seek and long for the presence of our beloved. Seek the face of the Lord. This is meditation. Meditation is not meant to be a discipline, a rigorous exercise of the mind set quite apart from the joy of daily living in Christ; it is meant to be a time within the whole way of life in union with God, within the whole "life style" of a Christian, in which one intensifies, deepens and consolidates the relationship with God. Here we listen more attentively and share more reflectively the ongoing dialogue of the day with the Lord. And then we rest in him. Liturgy and contemplation do not stand as contrasting realities but as integral parts of the union they intend. With or without a "system" of meditation, then, content need not be concocted, "thought up," removed from the situation where Jesus meets us this day. But *this day's* work of the Lord which has called forth our praise through the liturgy can become our meditation.

Wouldn't it seem strange to you if someone decided to meditate on Easter Sunday with the theme of the Sacred Heart? Why not meditate on the nativity on Pentecost Sunday? Why not meditate on the raising of Lazarus on Christmas? The usual problem of distractions *in* prayer would never be a problem then, for the prayer itself, the very life style, would be a total distraction. Disjointed, discordant, disruptive, disunified elements should never be in our prayer life. Our God is a God of peace and order.

How well we have learned this in conducting our prayer meetings! We listen closely to the words Paul addresses to the Corinthians and to us about order, confusion and life in the Spirit. Prayer meetings, as we all know, are closely related to and strongly resemble the Word service of the eucharistic liturgy in form and in structure. They are "paraliturgical" gatherings of people who come together explicitly to hear and share the Word of God. Some people say that they can pray *only* at Mass or at prayer meetings. They find the presence, gifts and fruits of the Spirit fading in daily life. This must grieve the Spirit. Every prayer meeting is modeled on the liturgy. If we would allow the liturgy to form our daily prayer life, we would find an amazing thing happening. The fruits of the Spirit, the full range of ministry gifts and praise and presence of God so vibrant in our communal celebrations, would begin to fill our whole week, each day, and every hour. We must learn in this way to let every day be a prayer meeting in miniature.

It is here in the community gathering, our prayer meetings, that the Lord has shown us many insights into spirituality. Foremost among these insights is our growing awareness of the necessity of the communal dimension in the spiritual life. The highly developed spirituality of the Middle Ages was always essentially rooted within communal life, since it had its origins within monastic life. It is the danger and the tendency of recent spirituality to be far too individualistic, to be far too concerned with the direction of one man to another man quite apart from a common life in Christ. What the pentecostal movement offers in terms of spiritual direction is a restoration of communal discernment and guidance. The Spirit moves within the community and the whole community experiences growth. Personal spirituality ceases to be isolated, but as growth occurs within members of the body it is "ministered" to one another. To be led by the Spirit in this way does not mean that people should not also have one spiritual director. But the imposition of abstract rules on an individual, particularly if the director does not share the community experience that underlies the whole development of an individual's growth, can be a form of advice and guidance that is far removed from where the Spirit is leading.

Coming together frequently, we interact in the power of the Holy Spirit to build each other up through the ministry gifts, through individual and communal discernment of prayer and the promptings of the Spirit, and through pastoral direction and guidance. Within the body of Christ, our experience in such uncharted realms as visions, sensory anointings, dreams, and prophecy can be tested and can find guidance and direction. All this ensures solid and steady growth in the life of the Holy Spirit of God. For it is only in the Church, and in prayer groups as intense manifestations of the body of Christ, that we can avoid the possibility of being led by a spirit that may well be our own.

It is true that the Holy Spirit will lead us and teach us—but we should never become so individualistic in our spiritual outlook that we fail to see the way in which the Spirit has been teaching and leading the whole Church of which we are a part. Let us rejoice in our charismatic renewal. Let us give praise for this impetus to a deepened spiritual life. And let us allow the insights of our "pentecost" to enrich and enliven our life and the life of the whole people of God in the Spirit. We share that Christ-life now with each other. We can share also in the spiritual heritage of saints and scholars whose writings and lives cry out the truth most fully expressed and realized in the liturgy of the eucharist: Christ has died, Christ is risen, Christ will come again!

Baptism in the Holy Spirit and the Mystic Way

Susan B. Anthony

Midway in my life's journey, I lay convalescing from an illness in a cottage high over the Caribbean in Jamaica, in the West Indies. Staring at the bright-burning pimento wood fire that was warming my bedroom against a February norther, I was wondering why my life had been so filled with disasters, trials by fire, flood, wreck and even violence. Why was I finding not peace, but a sword? Why had my prayers led to not bread but a stone?

Dimly I recalled Dante's *Inferno* and *Purgatorio,* and the forty days and nights of Jesus in the wilderness. Dimly I recalled the words purgatory, purging, cleansing, purification. These words came to me as I lay in my bed looking up at the cathedral-like ceiling of the cottage, once the kitchen building of the plantation, blackened by the fireplace cooking of 200 years. Was it possible, I wondered, that these trials I had undergone showed that I, Susan, needed a cleansing, a purification, a mortification even? But my mind recoiled at such a thought; after all, I knew I had already had a spiritual awakening to a Higher Power. What more could I possibly need? My daily prayers of petition should be the answer to all my problems. And yet, as I lay in the cedar bed next to the fire, I sensed that, somehow, spiritual awakening is not enough. It could be that spiritual awakening might be just the beginning. Maybe I needed to do more than wake up to the truth that there is a Higher Power, a God. Maybe I needed to strip, to throw out the old fears, the old hates, the stale ideas which had festered, fed on me, and erupted and all but destroyed me. Maybe I must cleanse myself of the bondage to dubious excitement that had been my life as a reporter for years. And there was another bondage, a bondage of desire, the compulsive desire for my will and my way—I want what I want when I want it.

It had taken me thirty years of living to heed God's goad to spiritual awakening. I had delayed since then, perhaps recognizing my need to cleanse, to purify, to detach myself from fear, frustration, resentment, and compulsive self-will. Since I had failed to take the initiative in cleansing, God had permitted these trials and disasters.

Back in college in my freshman year, though an honor student in the social sciences and English, I had nearly flunked biology. I simply couldn't understand all those boring little creatures, amoebas, frogs or crayfish. To me they were just annoying trifles in a maze of microscopes, slides and tweezers. Had I seen biology not as a series of unrelated experiments, had I seen it as the fabulous evolution of living matter moving from the simplest of single cells to the complex climax we call man, I might even have excelled in biology.

Now as I lay in my bedroom with its bare cut-stone walls, its grilled window so much like a cell in some ancient monastery, it came to me: there just might be an evolution of the soul. Perhaps the inner self must go through an evolution, just as does the biological self!

These trials, these disasters and this suffering might be a cleansing to prepare me for a further step in the evolution of the soul. Perhaps spiritual awakening was the first step toward a further breakthrough of the soul. And there I stopped, for I didn't know what the journey's end might be. My then religion in a non-Christian denomination had trained me only for the acquisition of goods, spiritual and material. My glimpses of God, sporadic and far apart in time, seemed to have no pathways to or from them. They came and they went, disappearing in the noise of my own typewriter, and in the disasters I reported and the violence of my own life.

I had nothing, no one to look up to or hold on to. The vague impersonal God of my then religion seemed lacking, unsatisfactory. It could not help me.

Eighteen months later I was grounded again in my motor-minded reporter's life and stayed at home with a cold. Idly I picked out a book I had bought two years earlier in New York but had left unread in our home-made ceiling-high cedar bookshelves. It was Evelyn Underhill's great classic *Mysticism,* written way back in 1910. I started reading it that day in June, 1959. I have really never stopped reading it since. For in the second half of the book lay the anatomy of the interior journey to God taken by the great mystics of many religions. But I noticed to my surprise that most of them were Catholic saints, even though Underhill herself was an Anglican, not a Roman. What excited me in her book was that where I had stopped in my journey, she began. She opened her book with the spiritual awakening of the self; then she took me with her pure prose to the purification of the self, then to the illumination that comes with prayer leading to contemplation, through the dark night of the soul to the climax of unconditional surrender, and finally to the goal, the end, the term that she called the unitive state. So beautifully did the mystic-theologian-poet present these stages in the interior life that I was unaware she was leading me to accept the language of Christianity. Oddly enough I found the language of the Christian contemplatives not too difficult. Eagerly I read on, digesting the interior way, the stages the ardent soul passes through on its journey to union. And during those two days of reading and meditation, seeds were sown whose ultimate flowering I could not even imagine.

She called this journey the mystic way, stating: "Mysticism then is not an opinion; it is not a philosophy. It has nothing in common with the pursuit of occult knowledge. It is not merely the power of contemplating Eternity. . . . It is the name of that organic process which involves the perfect consummation of the love of God: the achievement here and now of the immortal heritage of man. Or, if you like it better—for this means exactly the same thing—it is the art of establishing his conscious relation with the Absolute." And she further said: "The mystic knows his task to be the attainment of Being, union with the One, the 'return to the Father's heart,' for the parable of the prodigal son is to him the history of the universe."

Defining the mystic himself, she said: "The mystics —to give them their short, familiar name—are men and women who insist that they know for certain the presence and activity of that which they call the love of God. They are conscious of that Fact which is there for all, and which is the true subject-matter of religion, but of which the average man remains either unconscious or faintly and occasionally aware."

Still bogged down in the quagmires of my own external troubles, I began to pray that God would lead me out of purgation to the next stage of the mystic way—illumination. I had already moved from solely prayers of petition to increasing hours spent in meditation. I did not, however, voluntarily undergo any further cleansing. Again it was taken out of my hands and I was forced to the first real surrender of my life, which meant giving up my entire life in Jamaica. I embarked on what I called a "spiritual sabbatical," first for sheer survival, only secondarily for my search for God's illumination.

Then it was in a little upper room—stripped of status, alone and broke, with no prospects or plans— that the event happened that was to change my life. I looked around at the lonely, bare, little room, and out at the rain-washed street below. Instead of feeling sorry for myself, however, a great feeling of sorrow for a past hurt I had dealt my mother came up and smote me, bringing a flood of tears that melted me into contrition. That moment of contrition led instantly to a letter of amends, of apology. I begged for forgiveness. I typed out the envelope and placed the letter in it. As I sealed it, the forgiveness came. I knew I was forgiven. I knew that I was forgiven by my mother. As I sealed the envelope, I knew that I was forgiven by another Person, the Person of Jesus Christ. In that split and blinding second I knew that Jesus was not just a man, he was God. I stood up. I went to the window. I turned. And he said:

"I am God. Before Abraham was, I am."

He held out his arms. "Come unto me . . . and I will give you rest."

I answered as I surrendered to him, "Yes, Lord, yes."

That momentous day began my real illumination— my life in Christ. Though totally insecure in my external life, I was blissfully certain and secure in my interior life. My Lord led me every step of the way, led me right into the Catholic Church, where he had first given the teaching of the interior journey. The Catholic Church has been the repository of the mystic way through her saints, teachers, and writers, since he first taught and exemplified the way in its fullness.

Two months after my confirmation in the Church, I knelt in earnest prayer after communion. Then it was that I learned of the third Person of the Blessed Trinity. God the Holy Spirit came to me without warning in a way least expected. He made himself known in a completely formed verse. This was my first meeting with the Lord and giver of Life, the beginning of my devotion to the Holy Spirit.

But as a brand new Catholic in the year of our Lord 1961, I soon found that devotion to the Holy Spirit was devotion to the forgotten Person of the Blessed Trinity.

Though I searched for him everywhere in my studies of theology, he seemed strangely neglected.

I searched for him in current literature. I looked for the symbol of the dove in Catholic bookstores. He seemed absent. I could buy a thousand books on our Lady, a thousand medallions of the saints, but it took a friend of mine one year to find for me a suitable symbol of the Holy Spirit for my desk. It almost seemed as though the descent of the dove had never taken place.

But he continued to guide, direct and teach me. Most important, he gave me more and more prayer that I knew was not my own, lifting my own spirit as the clouds built up in the fast-approaching dark night. He led me to give my utmost in time and energy to the practice of prayer. Often I would drop on my knees in the Loretto Chapel at Saint Mary's, look up at the shining iridescent symbol of him in the steeple and beg him during arduous tasks and trials: "Please, Holy Spirit, you take over."

I walked at least a half hour in the forest each day waiting for him. I read everything I could find in Scripture, in the Church's teachings and in theology about him. He wrote a prayer through me, dedicated to him, called, "The time that is left belongs solely to you." I even named my little cottage in his honor, Casa de la Paloma. I soon filled it with not only books on him, but doves in painting, in metal, in mobiles.

Then a dark night descended upon my outer and inner life. I entered a period of external crises that called upon every resource in my experience to carry me through. I truly learned to live one day at a time. I truly learned to rely on Jesus only. In prayer I would often gaze at the crucifix on my wall. It was a bronze dove descending on a black lead cross. The dove was superimposed on the cross. As I gazed at it I was led to believe: "The Spirit transcends the cross."

The dove on the cross led me to hope that he would

guide me through the tunnel of the dark night. He added that I must yield still more to him, even my tongue. I began to seek the baptism in the Holy Spirit through prayers said by clergy and laymen, individually and in prayer groups. I included in my own daily prayer discipline the golden sequence of the Church, asking for this further step. For years I had practiced mental prayer walking in forests, or in these last five years by the sea, readying myself to receive, as the Lord willed, his contemplation in me. Some of these glimpses of him have been absolutely wordless. I had no way of knowing when he would grant these wordless moments. All I could do was prepare for them by thanksgiving, petition, and meditation. When I have been faithful in my prayer life, and when I have gotten my self out of the way, my word-making machine stopped and I merely gazed at him with wordless love. Afterwards I rejoiced and savored the experience and prayed it would happen again.

One month after I began praying specifically for the infilling or baptism in the Spirit, I was led to take my prayer-walk on a dark and rainy night. As I walked and prayed I heard children singing in a nearby house. It came to me that the children were praising God in sing-song unknown tongues. At that moment I let go, and I began to praise the Lord in sounds that did not come from my mind, to a tune that I did not compose. Out came a song of praise in a new tongue. I thanked God and asked him what I had never asked before. I asked for a sign confirming that this was truly the Holy Spirit praying in me, and not just my willed human expression. I searched the darkness, even though I knew that my usual "seagoing doves of the Spirit," the sea gulls, would not be flying at night. But I persevered in prayer as I walked on the hard, wet sand by the sea.

Suddenly the clouds parted on the black horizon to the east, and there shone, soaring like the dove, the heavenly constellation called the "Kite." The dove had made a breakthrough in the dark night. It was my confirmation that the Spirit had indeed filled me. It was, I knew, a major step toward the final surrender guarding the narrowest gate of all, the gate to union with God. I did not make the mistake of presuming that I had entered the narrow gate to the final goal. Rather, I knew that I had received a great empowering, an activization by and of the Spirit to carry me the rest of the way. In common with all Christians I had received in my soul sacramentally at baptism the Holy Spirit and the first and second Persons of the Trinity. Then he came to dwell in me as love, as grace, and as the sanctifier. His special mission of love within the Trinity is to bring us all to sanctity, or unconditional love. He is the author and director of each Christian at all stages of the mystic way. But he becomes the actor, the dominating, active presence within the soul, only when the soul attains union.

In receiving this charismatic gift—tongues—I had received an important addition to my prayer life; it was also a sign that I had surrendered at least sufficiently for this gift. Even more momentous to me, the event signified the beginning of the end of the dark night of the soul. I think that some who have received the baptism in the Holy Spirit believe that it is the end and goal of the spiritual journey. Actually it occurs more commonly at the beginning, after the central religious experience, the conversion to the Person of Jesus Christ as Savior. Many Catholics who have encountered Jesus personally for the first time move right on to the further infilling of the Holy Spirit. Or it can occur when we are on the purgative way, voluntarily or involuntarily cleansing our lives, setting them in order to conform to Christ. The empowering of the Spirit can accelerate the purgative stage, telescope it to some extent, leading us to the illuminative state more quickly. Or it can happen as it did to me at a time when the Spirit had

already begun contemplation in me and I had descended
to the dark night.

Whenever it takes place, the baptism in the Holy
Spirit can be of enormous value to a Christian committed to the conscious attainment of union with God.
The essential nature of our act in the event is a yielding,
a surrender. As such it enhances our docility to the Spirit,
the author and director of our holiness. The charismatic
gifts which may follow, however, are accidents, not the
substance of our sanctification. And they are primarily
for the building of the body of Christ, not for personal
sanctification, even though they may be used toward that
goal. In this sense the surrender to the Spirit provides an
activization of him, leading to a great leap toward the
goal. It could even bring us to the unitive state. More often, however, it is a transient act of surrender, not the
state of total self-abandonment required for the final union.

A second major effect of the baptism in the Holy
Spirit is in the individual's prayer life. The liberation of
praying "in the Spirit" leads to liberation of praying in
English. Many Catholics who never said a spontaneous
word to God in their lives are now praying freely and
beautifully to him. Rote prayers are fast disappearing
among pentecostal Catholics who use their own heartfelt
words to maintain that "frequent and solitary converse
with him who we know loves us." The Holy Spirit accomplished in the American Catholic Church in one
year, 1967–1968, what human effort could not achieve in
four years of hard work at spontaneous prayer conferences at Saint Mary's, Notre Dame, Marymount College,
Boca Raton, and elsewhere. Once Pentecost descended
upon the leaders in the Middle West, a revival in spontaneous prayer swept the country in the Church, including a revival in the Christian practice of healing prayer.

The Holy Spirit did not stop here. As author of contemplation, he has even led some Catholic pentecostals from the earlier prayer stages of petition and meditation to the goal of contemplation. Though praying in tongues is not of itself contemplation, it can be and often is a step to the lasting knowledge of God for the person. As one who believes that contemplation is for everyone, and not just for the elite, this to me is one of the finest contributions of the pentecostal movement to the Church. One visit to a Catholic pentecostal prayer meeting shows how the Spirit is leading ordinary Catholics to the loving, experiential knowledge of Jesus Christ and the Trinity. Some Spirit-filled Catholics already practice the presence of God twenty-four hours a day.

Finally, the infilling of the Spirit helps us persevere to the goal through the gift of healing prayer. For we can use the charism of healing prayer toward this greatest of all healings, the union of our will with God, for ourselves and others. We can also use the gift of healing prayer to combat the adversary who becomes intimately revealed to most of us who receive the baptism of the Holy Spirit.

But even the presence of the Holy Spirit within us is not the final goal of union with God. He is the forerunner preparing us for the end goal, which is our identification with Jesus Christ. St. Paul expressed it in Galatians 2, 20, saying: "It is no longer I who live, but Christ who lives in me."

Jesus, our Lord, is our witness to what we should witness. In seeking union with the whole Christ, we seek to emulate him. The goal of Christian mysticism, as distinct from Eastern mysticism, is to follow in his steps. Those steps lead up to the mountain of prayer to the Father. But they also lead down to the marketplace with our fellow man. The Eastern mystic is content to remain in the arms of the Beloved on the mountain; not so the Christian. Following our Lord, we unite with him while uniting with our brothers. Divine fecundity, bearing and rearing children of the Spirit, is the second aspect of our two-way life. We rest with our love while being sent by him to minister to our brothers. The Christian mystic is the prayer-supported apostle, identifying with Christ and sent by him to the corner of the world that calls him—the university, the ghetto, the hospital, the migrant camp, the alcoholic or drug-addict meeting, the typewriter, the kitchen, everywhere.

Jesus, in gathering the apostles, founded the first prayer-share teaching group. It has been the model for all effective spiritual action ever since. The validity of the Catholic pentecostal movement is shown at its best in the mushrooming of these fellowship-in-depth groups throughout the country. We are truly following in his steps when we come together to improve our communion with him, while sharing our communion with our brothers. Though we are active members of the larger fellowship, the Church, we, like Christ, need the small prayer-share group where we can informally and intimately move in love and prayer from a kinship of our suffering to a kinship of our sanctity.

In our suffering century we need the love of Christ and the love of each other, not for salvation alone but for sheer survival. The history of our planet shows that there is no geographical cure, no political or economic cure, for the basic problem of mankind. Kingdoms, dictatorships and democracies come and go. Empires and economic systems rise and fall. These external accidents of man's history have not given and cannot give to the individual person interior life, interior liberty, or the pursuit of happiness. History has shown that wholesale, large-scale political and economic reforms and revolutions simply do not heal the interior ills that plague us. Psalm 146 warns us:

> Do not put your trust in men in power,
> or in any mortal man—he cannot save;

> he yields his breath
> and goes back to the earth he came from,
> and on that day all his schemes perish.

The men in power may be president, prime minister or generalissimo. They are human and their schemes are fallible. Only the prince of peace, Jesus Christ, can give to our species survival and salvation. He told us the way: "Set your hearts on his kingdom first, and on his righteousness, and all these other things will be given you as well" (Mt. 6, 33).

Power To Witness

Leon and Virginia Kortenkamp

One of the last things that those who have had the baptism in the Spirit need to be convinced of is the need for Christian witness. It seems to be universally true that those who have come into this experience are taught not so much by one another but by the direct power of God, that every tongue (including theirs) is meant to proclaim that Jesus is Lord. We knew previously that we should proclaim the Gospel of Jesus with our lives, but now we realize that full proclamation of the lordship of Jesus must be more than a social conscience in the world, more than an affirmation of the brotherhood of man, or the need for world peace, or the need for all social barriers among men to be broken down. Pentecostals experience a new conviction that the Gospel must be proclaimed, studied, and taught, because it is Jesus who is the Alpha and the Omega. We have experienced the impact of the injunction to "seek first the kingdom of God and his justice and the rest shall be given." And so we "cannot but speak the things which we have seen and heard." Besides, this has been a new realization (though for some just a deeper realization); it has meant for many, ourselves included, a complete reversal of priorities and thought patterns.

Before the baptism in the Holy Spirit, we were convinced that the best way to proclaim the Gospel was never by word of mouth. The Gospel was just to be lived.

If anything was to be talked about, it was living a Christian life. We felt hostile to the thought of anything more direct than that. We found that the Lord can change both hearts and minds: "I tell you most solemnly, when you were young you put on your own belt and walked where you liked; but when you grow old you will stretch out your hands, and somebody else will put a belt round you and take you where you would rather not go" (Jn. 21, 18–19).

Several weeks after the baptism in the Holy Spirit, we became aware that our behavior and thoughts on the matter had changed completely. We can imagine the smiles of those readers who experienced the same thing. The hearts of many persons have been changed by this new seriousness and new love toward Jesus who is the one Savior of us all. "What greater peril is there for the world than not to receive Christ?" asks St. Hilary. The question has burned itself in our consciences.

There is nothing wrong, nothing un-Christian, about living the social doctrines of Jesus. We all must. The Bible teaches it explicitly. It also teaches us that something essential is lacking in our Christian lives if that is all we do, since Christianity is not a set of rules, a formula for life, a philosophy, a love-ethic; it is a conscious and growing personal relationship with God himself, one God in three Persons to be known and loved. He is not an impenetrable mystery, a triangle signifying three-in-one, a set of one-two-three principles, a first cause; he is not my wife, my husband, or my friends (or even me). There is an essential difference between life lived after the pattern of Jesus' life and life lived *in* Jesus. It is the difference between knowing about a person and knowing the person.

Jesus wants us to know him and to know about him. Nearly all of us have struggled with the impossibility of trying to love when we only knew about the Lord. The command, "You shall love the Lord your God with your whole heart, with your whole soul, with your whole mind, and with all of your strength" left us cold. Its significance was in the fact that it was a command from God, rather than an authentic response from us to him. Jesus wants men to come to him and to know him. He is the good news, and we are debtors when it comes to the good news. We owe him to the world because he belongs to the world. St. Paul says, "To the Greeks and the barbarians, to the wise and to the unwise, I am a debtor" (Rom. 1, 14). And the Lord says, "Feed my sheep" and "As the Father sent me so I am sending you" (Jn. 20, 21–22). In St. Mark's gospel he says, "Follow me and I will make you into fishers of men" (Mk. 1, 17) and "Go out to the whole world; proclaim the good news to all creation" (Mk. 16, 16). Paul, in writing to Timothy, exclaims, "So you are never to be ashamed of witnessing to the Lord" (2 Tm. 1, 8), and he exhorts the Corinthians: "We will have none of the reticence of those who are ashamed, no deceitfulness or watering down the Word of God, but the way we commend ourselves to every human being with a conscience is by stating the truth openly in the sight of God. If our Gospel does not penetrate the veil, then the veil is on those who are not on the way to salvation, the unbelievers whose minds the god of this world has blinded, to stop them seeing the light shed by the good news of the glory of Christ, who is the image of God. For it is not ourselves that we are preaching, but Christ Jesus as Lord" (2 Cor. 4, 2–6).

Cardinal Suenens adds a voice of encouragement to us regarding the necessity of a direct apostolate, reflecting the same direction and the same sense of urgency seen in the documents of Vatican Council II. Suenens says, "No one has the right to stand aside on the pretext that he has but one talent and prefers to bury it in the earth. Each must give the full measure of the grace that is in him."

One-to-One Ministry

Isaiah 40, 3–5 states:

A voice that cries in the wilderness:
Prepare a way for the Lord,
make his paths straight.
Every valley will be filled in,
every mountain and hill be laid low;
winding ways will be straightened
and rough roads made smooth.
And all mankind shall see the salvation of God.

Preparation for one-to-one ministry begins with our one-to-one relationship with the Father through Jesus himself. This is the way the Lord has shown us by his own example. In receiving John's baptism, the baptism of repentance, Jesus showed us what our posture before the Father should be. We are to come to him acknowledging our complete dependence before him; we are to come in utmost humility, understanding that his life is a pure gift; we are to come to him admitting our weakness, our sin, and our inability to do anything without him. Then God can begin to deal with us as we really are, where we really are.

After his baptism by John, Scripture says that Jesus was led by the Spirit to a place away from everyone else where he fasted and prayed for forty days and forty nights. It was only after this preparation that Jesus began a public ministry. The principle involved should be our guide in one-to-one ministry: our life with the Lord must be maintained, constantly and faithfully, and we must speak to God about men before speaking to men about the Lord. Once we know what the Lord wants us to do, we need only claim the power of his Spirit to carry it out, relying completely on Jesus' promises about what the

Spirit would accomplish through us. A recollection of the first Pentecost should convince us of that. So we begin speaking about our Savior by listening—first to him and then to our brothers and sisters.

Listening to our brothers and sisters may involve asking questions, but, basically, "sounding the other out" in this way means to understand, to inquire with gentleness. The understanding should move on three lines in particular: (1) his readiness for change, (2) his present attitude, and (3) the circumstances in which his life goes on, in order to know specifically the opportunities for more and continued contact, the introduction to community life that he has had, and whether there are any serious occasions of sin that must first be eliminated before there can be an opening for God's Spirit to work.

The point of listening is learning how to love and how to let God love through us. To do this we need to understand not so much a person's position on "things" as his disposition regarding things of the Spirit. Through this kind of understanding we can see clearly and can judge, as our Lord would judge, just where we should begin and how we should proceed to make straight the path and to present the truth.

The sensitivity to and awareness of both the Spirit and the person require that we desire and pray that our speech always be an oracle of God. This may mean that we should begin to examine our patterns of conversation. It may mean that we should leave trivia out, and certainly it means that conversations marked by negativism and unruliness must be changed and renewed. It means that we should make of our conversations what God wants and not what we want. To converse "in the Spirit" does not mean that our conversation cannot be marked by the everyday. Rather, it means that we do not let the everyday become mundane. St. Paul makes the point clearly: "Be tactful with those who are not Christians and be sure you make the best use of your time with them. Talk to them agreeably and with a flavor of wit, and try to fit your answers to the needs of each one" (Col. 4, 5–6). If our everyday language is personal and always touched with eternal realities, the Spirit will have freedom to move because we are already speaking in tune with him.

To witness personally is sometimes difficult. It is easy to speak of ideas, and to keep ideas theoretical. But for most people, theory lacks life. To have life, theory has to intersect with life. One of the best ways to lend life to spiritual realities is to lend them our own lives—exactly what Jesus did in the incarnation, the Word made flesh!

Personal witness has another advantage. It keeps those who are so tempted from presenting an impersonal God—one who is held at arm's distance where he is under control. The problem of keeping God in his place is often unrecognized by those who suffer from it.

We all have natures rebellious against God, whether consciously or subconsciously. We all rebel against serving. We all would like to be our own gods, to be the most loved, the most sought after, the richest, to be the most admired, the best thought of, the one with the most friends, the one with the sharpest wit, the one with all the facts, the one with the most influence in the world (or maybe just in our own small world). In short, what we all want is homage paid to our egos, and in pursuing this end we proceed to dethrone our God and enthrone ourselves. It was Satan's enticement to Eve: "You shall be as gods." It is because our nature is the way it is that we have to decrease in order for the Lord to increase. Each of us has something or someone enthroned at the center of our lives. To make room for the Lord doesn't mean to make ready the extra bedroom or the extra chair; it means allowing him to reign from the center room, the very throne of our being. To have ourselves enthroned does not necessarily indicate we have our wills hardened against God, or for that matter even our hearts. The cause might be as simple as poor teaching or no teaching.

It might be what Billy Graham, in his book *World Aflame*, calls the problem of Christian immunization: a little bit of Christianity, like a little bit of live vaccine, is enough to keep those so "vaccinated" from ever getting the real thing—in this case, a conscious life with Jesus.

But whatever the cause, the act of love that is involved in personal witness carries with it the power of God which begins to undo all that needs undoing. The personal witness we can give to the fact that Jesus is Lord is unlike any other kind of witnessing, whether it be about toothpaste, laundry detergent, a car, or an interesting book we have just read. Witness to Jesus carries power—power to change men's hearts, power to change lives, power to enable men to experience life as really something, power to awaken and enkindle idealism, power to stir up hope and courage, power to lead men to hunger and thirst for a living life with our Lord. Witness to Jesus carries power because in it and through us he is the one who is calling to the others, calling as a lover. That attraction is not ours; it is his. The power is in our words, but it is his power. That is why it is absolutely essential that our lives be filled with his power if our words are to be. In his hands we are like bows, supple yet strong. And our words are as arrows, with the effect of arrows, because he pulled the string, and the power of the arrow now carries the power of him who loosed it.

The practical lessons we have learned through daily experience have taught us that witnessing usually takes the form of testimony about something God has done, either in us personally or in the lives of those around us. We may witness to the whole work God has done and is doing in our lives, or we may choose particular aspects of his work in us. As we describe the healing, forgiving, filling work that God has done in our lives, we bring others into immediate touch with the great truths of God's mercy.

It is important to bear in mind that giving testimony to our union with God is done for the edification of others. We should not run over our experiences of God again and again to relive experiences merely for our own good. If we are sharing our Christian lives in such a way that we draw attention to ourselves rather than to God, we must change the direction of our witness. We are to be witnesses of Jesus Christ, not of ourselves. If we feel a constant need to seek out someone to whom to tell our testimony in order to feel spiritually alive, we should seek direction about spiritual growth so that we can respond to the new and deeper life that lies ahead in the Lord.

If there are characteristics of our conversion, our baptism in the Holy Spirit, or other experiences of God which are extremely personal or unusual, many times it is best that we explain them in a very general way. Sometimes being too specific only distracts from the real action of God and draws attention to particular circumstances and to ourselves. We must always encourage others to realize that salvation is for all persons and that God makes no exceptions in his love for men. To be too particular about circumstances or about the uniqueness of our personality could lead another person to conclude that these unusual circumstances or our unique personality are the reasons that God has moved so noticeably in our lives and are thereby impossible conditions to his movement in another life.

For example, someone may have had a problem with alcohol, or an even deeper problem of a bitter, cynical attitude toward religion, before knowing Jesus Christ as his personal Savior. If this person, in describing the experience of God's mercy in his life, went into vivid detail concerning his life before knowing Jesus Christ, he could so cloud and condition the experience of God that much of the real depth and presence would be lost. Or another person might share in detail an unusual awareness of God's presence experienced during prayer. It is best if descriptions of our awarenesses of God during prayer are made very general. Of course, again, if we do share experiences we have during prayer, we should share only things which are given to us for sharing to bring others to know God and not to draw attention to our prayer life and its particular characteristics.

Since our testimony of God's life in us is a powerful means of drawing others to know God, it makes sense to spend some time and energy preparing ourselves to do this work of love the best way possible. Prayerful reflection on our lives in the Lord and on Scripture can help us to understand with ever greater clarity exactly what truths of God's love for men are being lived out in us. Prayerful reflection is different from introspection. The latter is clearly self-centered, while the former is, through the guidance of the Holy Spirit and Scripture, a preparation to love.

A very practical preparation which can follow on prayerful reflection is that of putting our experiences into a form which is easily communicated, forming our experiences into stories which can be easily shared with another. The stories should be honest, simple and to the point. They should point to the truths of God's love which they illustrate. To have our "testimony" clearly understood in our own mind in the form of stories prepares us to witness effectively.

If we are well prepared we can easily use a story from our experience to illustrate a particular reality of the Gospel, suited to the recognized needs of the person to whom we are witnessing. In this way we can use all of our testimony or portions of it, stressing certain aspects or skipping over them according to the needs of the listener. We can share in private conversations or in a group.

Although giving testimony to those who have never known God should be an active part of every Christian life, there is more than that to witnessing. We are also called to witness to each other within the community of believing Christians. We are called to share in such a way that our witness will build up the body of Christ within the body itself.

As we examine our experiences and prepare for witnessing we should remember that any experience—from a dramatic conversion to the answer to a simple prayer—can become a powerful apostolic tool when shared in a story from which illustrates God's action. As we experience God through prayer, the sacraments, a lesson in Scripture, or our brothers and sisters in the community, we have many stories of God's action among men. Each story is another chance to build up someone's faith, to lead someone to greater hope, to participate in God's saving love.

As we have said before, personal witness is not and should not be, the end of one-to-one ministry. One-to-one ministry involves more of a commitment than just testimony; it should lead people through a series of steps to a definite destination: You, too, can know Jesus, for "it is with fear of the Lord in mind that we try to win people over" (2 Cor. 5, 11) . . . Do you want to? . . . The way is through repentence and acceptance of Jesus as a personal Savior . . . The baptism in the Holy Spirit will make your new life a dynamic force, "for we cannot but speak the things which we have seen and heard" (Acts 4, 20) . . . Let's join our hands and journey together "from glory to glory."

St. Paul's exhortation to his fellow workers gives us as much direction as inspiration to be steadfast in season and out: "As his fellow workers, we beg you once again not to neglect the grace of God that you have received. . . . We do nothing that people might object to, so as not to bring discredit on our function as God's servants. Instead, we prove we are servants of God by great fortitude in times of suffering: in times of hardship and distress; when we are flogged, or sent to prison, or mobbed; laboring, sleepless, starving. We prove we are God's servants by our purity, knowledge, patience and kindness; by a spirit of holiness, by a love free from affectation; by the word of truth and by the power of God; by being armed with weapons of righteousness in the right hand and in the left, prepared for honor or disgrace, for praise or blame; taken for imposters while we are genuine; obscure yet famous; said to be dying and here we are alive; rumored to be executed before we are sentenced; thought most miserable, yet we are always rejoicing; taken for paupers, though we make others rich, for people having nothing, though we have everything" (2 Cor. 6, 1–10).

When Paul says in the above text that we should do nothing to which people might object, it should be clear that he is not referring to witnessing to Jesus but rather to our own personal conduct. Stressing the importance of being steadfast in faith and trust as witnesses to our Lord, Paul reminds us that there will be much required of us, much to go through, but that we need never go under. We continue, putting all else aside, simply because we believe, and the one in whom we believe is faithful to us in all things. As St. Paul says: "I believed and therefore I spoke" (2 Cor. 4, 13).

Catholics and Pentecostals Meet in the Spirit

Kevin M. Ranaghan

The main ballroom of the Beverly Hilton Hotel in Los Angeles was jammed with close to 3,000 Christians, and an unnumbered radio audience was listening in over KHOF. This provided a dramatic setting for a small but significant act of love. It was July 1968, and I had been speaking at the international convention of the Full Gospel Business Men's Fellowship, presenting an historical-theological résumé of the charismatic renewal in the Catholic Church, along with my personal testimony. Later, a perfectly normal looking man in a business suit came up to the microphone. With a genuine tremor in his voice he told of his previous conviction that no Catholic could be his brother in Christ. He remarked how his background and environment as a convert from Judaism to Christianity in a pentecostal church had made him sure that no practicing Catholic could really be a Christian; that Catholicism, "having no part in Christ," was deserving of a hatred reserved for the works of Satan. But tonight, he said, that false vision was dissolved; he had recognized in this Catholic who had spoken, the life of Jesus and the power of the Holy Spirit. Then he asked me to join him at the podium and there he embraced me in the love of Christ, saying all the while that he never had thought to see such a miracle.

114

I recall that in that moment I was oblivious to the several thousands in attendance and their chorus of approving "Amens." Rather, I was flooded again by the realization that through the charismatic renewal which we are experiencing, God is healing breaches and wounds in the body of Christ where they have never been able to be healed before. Walls of separation long dividing people equally loved by Christ and truly dedicated to him are beginning now by the action of the Spirit to crumble; fear, suspicion, ignorance, and hatred, are being dissipated in this vigorous and refreshing breeze.

The newly-found areas of relationship between Catholics and Protestants as a result of this outpouring of God's Spirit are by no means an insignificant aspect of the renewal we are experiencing. My encounter with a newly-found brother in Christ in Beverly Hills is but one example of hundreds of similar meetings with which I have been blessed in the past four years. More importantly, it is no exaggeration to say that the vast majority of Roman Catholics who are receiving the baptism in the Holy Spirit are continually finding mutual love and acceptance with Protestant pentecostals as brothers and sisters in Christ. In almost every prayer group, and certainly at every day of renewal, conference, or special meeting organized and carried on under the auspices of a Catholic charismatic prayer group, one can find numbers of classical and neo-pentecostal Christians who are participating in the meetings—not as a Protestant contingent, but very simply and unassumingly as our brothers and sisters in the body of Christ.

On the one hand, it is most important to note that this outpouring of the Holy Spirit in these days has occurred to Catholics within the Catholic Church. The charismatic renewal has not separated or excluded Catholics from the Church. Rather, it has renewed their love of the Church and has built up a lively faith within the Catholic community. While this "movement" is then authentically Catholic, it has brought about a new dimension in ecumenical relations. For centuries, walls of fear and distrust have been built between Christians of different denominations. To heal the scandal, the Churches in the last fifty years have entered ecumenical dialogue which at times has had wonderful results and at others has met with failure and frustration. Today, by the work of the Spirit among us, some of those old bricks have been knocked loose, and on a person-to-person level we are encountering each other for the first time in an experience of the love of Jesus. We now see Catholics, evangelicals, and fundamentalists sitting down together around the Word in a common experience of salvation to praise our Father with one voice in unity and love. Our unity is by no means complete. We still have many differences in doctrine and practice. But the unity we share in faith in Jesus, in praise of the Father, and in the life of the Holy Spirit is genuine. Thus, what we have been unable to accomplish by ourselves has been worked among us by the Holy Spirit.

One of the first published accounts of the charismatic renewal at the University of Notre Dame in the spring of 1967 made this observation: "To many it seemed incongruous that a movement previously associated with lower-class Protestantism and fundamentalism should take root in a Catholic university ablaze with the progressive light of the Vatican Council." Perhaps to no group of people was this situation more incongruous than to the Catholics at Duquesne and at Notre Dame who first received the baptism in the Holy Spirit. We had had our preconceived notions of classical pentecostalism, but it was perhaps a blessing in disguise that we didn't know in detail the life-style, dogmatics, and culture of traditional pentecostal life in America. For if we had had this knowledge, it might well have militated against the desire of the Lord that we be filled with his Holy Spirit.

An Initial Meeting

I can never forget that first beautiful encounter in which I participated as a "Catholic pentecostal," meeting for the first time with fundamental pentecostals. It was March 13, 1967, and a small group made up mostly of those who had received the baptism in the Holy Spirit the previous week, and a few newcomers, went to a prayer meeting in the home of Ray and Mabel Bullard in nearby Mishawaka, Indiana. Ray was then president of the South Bend Chapter of the Full Gospel Business Men's Fellowship International, an interfaith group of laymen who share the experience of the baptism in the Holy Spirit. We had heard of this group and thought it good to share our experience with them. If this charismatic renewal were merely a human fiction, or even a form of religiosity created out of the wills of men, I really believe it would have crumbled to dust that evening. Never would we have thought it possible for men and women so radically different from one another in numerous ways to unite in the love of Christ. Here we were: a group of Roman Catholics, formed in the spiritual, theological, and liturgical patterns of our Church, all university-trained intellectual types. The people with whom we were meeting were mostly from a fundamentalist background. They spoke with that scriptural and theological fundamentalism that was very foreign to us. Furthermore, the way they spoke and prayed, the types of hymns they sang —all of this was so different that at first it was very disturbing. On the natural level these cultural differences were more than enough to keep us far apart from each other. But in spite of all the personal differences, we were, Catholics and Protestants alike, enabled to come together in common faith in Jesus, to share our experience of the Holy Spirit and to worship our Father together.

That, it seems to me, was no human achievement. The Holy Spirit simply cut across those cultural barriers and united us as brothers and sisters in Christ. The joy of that first meeting, the wonder of the realization of a shared experience of the power of the Holy Spirit cutting right across denominational lines, has been repeated hundreds and thousands of times across the United States and Canada in the last four years. Everywhere we look, serious wounds in the body of Christ begin to heal, brothers and sisters in Christ begin to know eath other, begin to stand on tiptoe and to peer over those walls of separation only to recognize in each other the image of Jesus Christ.

From the freshness of this experience of love and union in Christ has flowed over and over again the growth of warm friendship and deep and continuing fellowship as we have continued to pray together, to serve each other, and together to be a witness to our Lord and Savior in the world we live in. The union of Catholic and Protestant pentecostals has been no passing fancy; to a great extent, it has been deepened and matured in Christ. We have shown and continue to show our ability to cooperate and to work together in a common program to promote the Gospel.

The Contribution of Protestant Pentecostals

One could not accurately relate the story of the outpouring of the Holy Spirit among Roman Catholics in the last four years without repeatedly pointing out the outstanding contribution of Protestant pentecostals (both classical pentecostals from the traditional pentecostal denominations and neo-pentecostals from within the historical Reformation Churches) to the charismatic renewal in the Roman Catholic Church. Not only has there been a shared unity and fellowship in the work of the Holy

Spirit in the last few years, but time and time again the
Lord has used the service of brothers and sisters in Christ
from denominations other than Roman Catholic to initiate, to nourish, and to mature the outpouring of the
Holy Spirit among Roman Catholics.

In our own experience in the community in South
Bend, it was particularly true at the beginning of our
charismatic renewal that we depended heavily not only
on the friendship and prayer, but also on the encouragement, pastoral guidance, and seasoned experience of Protestant pentecostals associated both with the Assemblies of
God and with the Full Gospel Business Men's Fellowship.
Roy Wead, then pastor of Calvary Temple in South Bend,
and his son Doug, while at first understandably stunned
that Roman Catholics were holding charismatic prayer
meetings at the university, nevertheless did not hesitate
to jump into the breach, offering their services to help us
to respond fully to the Lord's will for us. Their experience in the area of the spiritual gifts and of leading people into the baptism in the Holy Spirit was invaluable.
Ray Bullard, whom we mentioned above as president of
the "Full Gospel" chapter in South Bend, spared no
effort to bring together a number of fine Christians, mature in the life of the Holy Spirit, to give us assistance.
Ray's maturity and solidness was of great help to us
from the very beginning. He was obviously a man deeply
attached to the Word of God, a man of regular and disciplined prayer and fasting. I remember being very struck
at that first meeting in his home by his insistence on the
primacy of the fruits of the Spirit in our lives, as opposed to a kind of idolization or vain fascination with
the ministry gifts of the Holy Spirit. His words have come
back to us many times, and we have seen the truth and
the value of what he said. Of outstanding service to us
in the beginning was the ministry of Hobart Freeman
whose insight and reflection on living and acting by New
Testament faith set a tone for many of us that was to

have a great role to play in sustaining the charismatic renewal in its first six to twelve months in our area.

I do not mean to imply that through the services of these men we immediately adopted a thoroughly pentecostalist dogmatic or that we threw over in any sense at all our Catholic theological tradition. Nothing could be further from the truth. In fact, we regularly maintained certain strong differences of opinion and belief with these men who were serving us so generously. But they did bring to us some emphases of New Testament living which we either had not known or had not seen fully before that time, and for this we will be ever grateful. I think it would be accurate to say that in our own history in the South Bend community (and I believe that this pattern has repeated itself numerous times around the country) this service of Protestant pentecostals has had particular value in the nascent stages of the charismatic movement.

As a matter of fact, I cannot praise too highly the willingness of Protestant pentecostal leaders to step back after they have performed the services for us which the Lord has led them to perform and to allow the organic Catholic leadership, teaching, and pastoral function to emerge within the primarily Catholic groups. Happily we have found little evidence of a desire or effort on the part of Protestant pentecostals to build up their own denominations or fellowships or prayer groups through the Catholic charismatic renewal. They have not attempted to exploit the pentecostal movement among Catholics for the building up of their own works and interests. But they have been blessedly content to allow the leading of the Holy Spirit to take its own organic course within Catholic circles.

Besides ministers and lay leaders from the principal classical pentecostal denominations, we have also been aided by leaders and directors of a whole group of independent pentecostal ministries or team associations of ministers throughout the country. There are, of course, a great number of these—too numerous to mention. As one outstanding example, let me mention the California-based Inter-Church Renewal Ministries under the direction of Rev. Ray Bringham of Newhall, California. Ray and his associates have a very strong ministry in leading people from a variety of denominations to know the Lord, to accept him more fully, to receive the baptism in the Spirit and to begin walking in the Spirit. They conduct this service through a series of interdenominational meetings, usually held in public places such as restaurants, simply for the spiritual good of the individuals with whom they are dealing, and with no desire of building up an organization or a counter church. Ministries such as these have been very helpful at the beginning of the charismatic renewal in a given area, or in leading individuals to the beginning of a new life in the Spirit.

To my mind, however, without a doubt the greatest Protestant pentecostal contribution to the charismatic renewal in the Catholic Church has come through the agency of the Full Gospel Business Men's Fellowship International. This organization was founded in 1953 by a California dairyman, Demos Shakarian. He was struck by the absence of men in the Protestant denominations in America, including the pentecostal denominations. In prayer, and under the guidance of the Lord, he came to see a vision of vast numbers of American men, coming to know, to witness to the Lord, and to fullness of life in the Holy Spirit. With this in mind, he and a group of associates began the F.G.B.M.F.I. as a men's fellowship which would seek in regular public meetings, by sharing the testimonies and experiences of ordinary Christian businessmen, to attract large numbers of men to the Lord. The organization from the very beginning was international, having hundreds of chapters throughout the United States, Canada, and the rest of the world. It is not a Church, nor is it related to any particular

Church organization. In some chapters the membership comes largely from the classical pentecostal denominations, with just a smattering of neo-pentecostals. In other chapters, however, it is difficult to find members of pentecostal denominations, but one can find rather large numbers of neo-pentecostals from Lutheran, Episcopalian, Presbyterian and Baptist backgrounds. While actual membership in the fellowship is restricted to businessmen, its meetings are always open to the public. The F.G.B.M.F.I. considers itself to be an arm of the Church, in the service of local churches and in no sense an attempt to lead people away from churches to which they would normally belong. It is therefore an independent service organization which seeks to facilitate the proclamation of the Gospel on the gutsy level of the businessman, and to lead people to desire, to seek and to receive the baptism in the Holy Spirit. On this level it is very strong, and the service it performs is performed by no one else quite as well. On the other hand the Full Gospel Business Men's organization by its very nature does not attempt, nor does it accomplish, continual, sustained, in-depth teaching or guidance or pastoral care for those who receive the baptism in the Spirit through its agency.

From the very beginning of the charismatic renewal among Roman Catholics, the Full Gospel Business Men have shown active interest and support and a great deal of generosity in promoting the baptism in the Holy Spirit among Roman Catholics. They have made it possible for me and for a number of other individuals with a sense of pastoral responsibility toward the movement as a whole to travel throughout the whole of the United States and Canada to speak to local chapters, to regional conventions, and to international conventions. In these situations one has the opportunity not only to share the common experience of the empowering of the Holy Spirit with Christians from a variety of denominations, but also to introduce newcomers from a variety of denominations, and especially newcomers who are Roman Catholics, to the good news of what the Lord is doing in our day through this outpouring of the Holy Spirit. While pentecostal culture, of which we will have much to say later on in this chapter, is usually very much in evidence in these meetings and might cause some newcomers to turn away precipitously, I think it is worthy of note that the F.G.B.M.F.I. has never entered into or supported the use of its platform for doctrinal or interconfessional polemics. On the contrary, their emphasis has been almost entirely on those things which unite Christians who confess the lordship of Jesus Christ and the desire to live in the life and the power of the Holy Spirit. Because of this their meetings have a great deal of openness, warmth, and love. Because they are not affiliated with any particular church, many people feel the freedom to come, to listen, to participate, and to respond to invitations for further instruction and prayer.

Numbers of Catholics throughout the United States and Canada who have responded positively to the invitation of a pentecostal friend to attend a "Full Gospel" meeting where there was a Catholic speaker have, through this ministry, not only come into the experience of the baptism in the Holy Spirit, but have furthermore been used by God in the establishment and nourishment of Catholic charismatic prayer groups in their own areas. Beyond the formal public meetings themselves, the F.G.B.M.F.I. is continually anxious to set up private meetings, seminars, clergy conferences and informal meetings of totally Catholic groups where inquiries can be made into the baptism in the Holy Spirit. These types of meetings have had the further advantage of not being fraught with the atmosphere of pentecostal or revivalistic culture. Finally, and perhaps most significantly, the meetings of the businessmen where Catholics have been the principal speakers have been tape recorded and duplicated by hundreds of people in attendance. These tapes have been circulated privately into homes, schools, and offices where Catholics at their own leisure have heard the good news of what the Lord is doing among us and have then been able in a very uninhibited way to respond to it themselves. This tape ministry which these meetings have made possible is, as far as I can see, one of the chief channels through which the experience of the baptism in the Holy Spirit and teaching on the life in the Spirit have been transmitted to hundreds and thousands of Catholics in the United States and Canada.

It is, of course, true that thousands and perhaps the majority of Catholics who have come into the charismatic renewal in the Church have entered it through the ministry of fellow Catholics rather than along ecumenical lines of fellowship with Protestant pentecostals. However, the Protestant witness to Catholics and their efforts to make Catholic testimony available to other Catholics have provided no small outlet for the good news of what the Lord is doing among us.

In the plan of God, our continued deep association with our Protestant pentecostal friends may take on different levels of intensity from place to place. While our friendship in Christ remains a constant joy, it is not altogether clear that we are called continually to work together in close association with each other, or to share one and the same prayer group, or to participate in precisely the same types of services to the public. In such areas we must cultivate a deep mutual respect, as well as a deep respect for the freedom of the Holy Spirit to move among us and direct us as he sees best. On the other hand, while the birth of the charismatic movement in the Catholic Church sprang directly from a rich Catholic tradition and an authentically Catholic hunger for more of the life of God, nevertheless the contribution of these Protestant pentecostal brethren, particularly in the areas of introductory witnessing, instruction and ministry, and in the sharing of the mistakes and errors in their own past experience, has been of immeasurable value at the very beginning of the Catholic charismatic movement.

Differences and Difficulties

We must first realize and accept on the deepest level the great gift that the Lord has given us in this new-found fellowship with brothers and sisters in Christ from denominational and neo-pentecostalism. They are genuinely our brothers and sisters in Christ. The degree of unity with which we have been blessed was foreseen by Vatican Council II as the genuine work of the Holy Spirit and as appropriate to the Church's view and understanding of the dimensions of the ecumenical movement. The *Decree on Ecumenism* reads: "Everywhere, large numbers have felt the impulse of this grace, and among our separated brethren also there increases from day to day a movement, fostered by the grace of the Holy Spirit, for the restoration of unity among all Christians. Taking part in this movement, which is called ecumenical, are those who invoke the triune God and confess Jesus Christ as Lord and Savior" (n. 2). Our experience with our pentecostal brothers and sisters in Christ has left us no doubt that they are in a very deep sense genuinely Christian. In past years I have encountered a number of Roman Catholics who, closed or opposed to the charismatic renewal in the Church, would raise the question of the authenticity of the Christianity of the pentecostal people. In response to this, one need only to cite the same Decree: "However, one cannot impute the sin of separation to those who at present are born into these communities and are instilled therein with Christ's faith. The Catholic Church accepts them with respect and affection as brothers. For men who believe in Christ and have been properly baptized are brought into certain, though imperfect, communion with the Catholic Church. . . . All those justified by faith through baptism are incorporated into Christ. They therefore have a right to be honored by the title of Christian, and are properly regarded as brothers in the Lord by the sons of the Catholic Church" (nn. 3–4).

Immediately the Council goes on to emphasize the point that we can expect and look for edification, for help in the general building up of our own Christian lives, from the example and contribution of Christians separated from the Catholic Church: "Moreover some, even very many, of the most significant elements or endowments which together go to build up and give life to the Church herself can exist outside the visible boundaries of the Catholic Church: the written Word of God; the life of grace; faith hope and charity, along with other interior gifts of the Holy Spirit and visible elements. All of these, which come from Christ and lead back to him, belong by right to the one Church of Christ. . . . Catholics must joyfully acknowledge and esteem the truly Christian endowments from our common heritage which are to be found among our separated brethren. It is right and salutary to recognize the riches of Christ and virtuous works in the lives of others who are bearing witness to Christ, sometimes even to the shedding of their blood. For God is always wonderful in his works and worthy of admiration. Nor should we forget that whatever is wrought by the grace of the Holy Spirit in the hearts of our separated brethren can contribute to our own edification. Whatever is truly Christian never conflicts with the genuine interests of the faith; indeed, it can always result in a more ample realization of the very mystery of Christ and the Church" (nn. 3–4).

Most Catholics participating in the charismatic renewal in the last four years, being blessed with fellowship in the Spirit with our Protestant pentecostal brethren, have come to experience these proclamations of the

Church in their day-to-day experience. But the Council
goes further; it is in no sense an attempt to hide or cover
over the very serious differences which may divide Christians of various denominations from the Roman Catholic Church. The Council never states that these differences
are unimportant, that they should be pushed to the background in an atmosphere of brotherhood and unity that
would be unrealistic. Repeatedly affirming our obligation
to affirm the Catholic faith as it has come to us from the
apostles, the Council calls us to study carefully those
points of difference and distinction between ourselves as
Roman Catholics and our Protestant brethren. "We must
come to understand the outlook of our separated brethren. Study is absolutely required for this, and should be
pursued with fidelity to truth and in a spirit of good will.
When they are properly prepared for this study, Catholics need to acquire a more adequate understanding of
the distinctive doctrines of our separated brethren as
well as of their own history, spiritual and liturgical life,
their religious psychology and cultural background" (n.
9).

In regard to our ongoing relationship with Protestant
pentecostals, I want to turn first to the subject of socio-
cultural and religio-cultural differences that exist between them as Protestant pentecostal communities and
ourselves as Roman Catholics. To a considerable extent
pentecostal culture involves among other things a certain
manner of speaking, a theological and prayer vocabulary,
a certain type of public behavior in group situations of
worship, sometimes a manner of dress, and to some extent certain elements of scriptural exegesis and moral
theology. The data of those areas have been transmitted
through a tradition imbedded in culture. Now if we
speak of pentecostal culture, we are hardly speaking of it
in a pejorative sense, nor are we attempting to make a
value judgment on it in itself. We would like, however,

to distinguish between what is essential to charismatic renewal in the life of the Church today (that is, the core experience of the baptism in the Holy Spirit, and the principles handed on to us by the Christian tradition for the nurturing and development of a deep and authentic life in the Spirit) and the cultural milieu in which it is taking place, whether Catholic or classical pentecostal.

We do this so that we can more clearly see the distinction between the life of the Spirit and any given cultural expression of the life of the Spirit. We do so lest we confuse the grace of God with the manifestation that the action of God will take among a specific group of people. To a considerable degree, classical pentecostal culture and Catholic culture (if we may use such terms) are different from each other in a variety of ways.

The grace of God, being intended for all men in all types of societies, moves transculturally, affecting men as they are, where they are. Pentecostal culture has certain roots and causes and reasons for development, and it is the authentic culture of the classical pentecostal people. It is the milieu in and through which the Lord has been dealing with them for several generations. It is authentically part of their life; it is genuinely their culture and must be respected as such. On the other hand, the cultural envelope in which they have received the baptism in the Holy Spirit, the ministry gifts of the Spirit and the ongoing life of the Spirit is precisely that: an envelope and not the essence of the experience itself. What we have been led to see in the charismatic renewal in the Church today is precisely the essence of renewal of life in the Holy Spirit.

What we are seeking is the empowering of the Holy Spirit of the risen Lord. We are seeking it, of course, as the people we are, as Catholic people, as products of the Catholic Christian tradition and culture. It would therefore be a grave mistake, a serious error, to think that in receiving the baptism in the Spirit one had or ought to seek to import classical pentecostal culture into the charismatic renewal in the Roman Catholic Church.

Cultural Distinctions

While this seems clear as a principle, in practice it often presents considerable difficulties. The pentecostal culture is rooted in the tradition springing from the beginnings of American revivalism in the late 18th century, which became a major national religious movement in the first two-thirds of the 19th century, and which became even further distinctive and radicalized in the holiness movement of the last third of the 19th century. The interdenominational revivals and camp meetings of this century, particularly those associated with the holiness movement, were inevitably mixed with and affected by the quality of rural American life in the face of the ruggedness and danger of the expanding frontier. Often rural and frontier in their style, the 19th- and 20th-century revivals were marked by bombastic preaching, by loud and emotional response, by spontaneous prayer, by an exhibitionist style, by displays of jumping, shouting, frenetic handclapping and near hysteria. Often with the revivals came a simplistic and individualistic Christian ethic. The righteous life was characterized by clean living; therefore no smoking, drinking, dancing, makeup, theater-going or other amusements were allowed. While it was considerably tempered over the last several decades, the revivalistic culture continues to pervade denominational pentecostalism. It is perhaps the gift box in which the gift comes to those people, but it should not be confused with the gift itself. In its own cultural setting and development, this religious style is quite beautiful, meaningful and relevant. But it is not essential to or desirable for the baptism in the Holy Spirit, especially among people of far different religious backgrounds. Pentecostals are often called "Holy Rollers" and advocates of the "old-time religion." It must be made clear that the social, cultural and doctrinal patterns of both Holy Rollers and the "old time religion" existed long before modern pentecostalism. The experience of the baptism in the Holy Spirit in contemporary Christianity was born into a pre-existing cultural pattern of behavior, and that cultural pattern of behavior which we call "pentecostal" culture has to a great extent been handed on almost as a sacred tradition within the ranks of pentecostals.

Today within pentecostalism one can find an authentic and powerful preaching of the Word of God, tremendous and genuine faith in Jesus Christ, and a very active life in the power of the Holy Spirit—all existing within a pattern which externally takes the form of an highly emotional and, to a considerable degree sometimes, an anti-intellectual form of preaching, teaching, and speaking.

Secondly, there exists a form of prayer language which is highly demonstrative and exuberant, while at the same time being deeply personal and revelatory of one's relationship with the Lord. This type of language is often accompanied by a coordinated body language which is quite foreign to those outside the pentecostal milieu. So, for example, prayers, while genuinely spontaneous, often contain the continued repetition of the name "Jesus," or the word "halleluia"; they are often accompanied by sobs or crying, by the raising of hands and arms and perhaps waving them around or clapping one's hands during prayer to give it emphasis, and, inasmuch as the prayer is communal, by urging others on with "amens" and "halleluias," which tend to raise emotional intensity.

There is a tendency in some of these communities to make the baptism in the Holy Spirit so paramount and central in the journey of the Christian through this world that an exclusivist type of language builds up around it, as when one might ask in inquiring about another person: "Have they received yet . . . ?" Or "Have they been blessed yet?" Or "Have they come into the experience yet?" This focus tends to obscure the validity, and in fact the necessity, for a variety of other elements in Christian life.

Pentecostal hymnody tends to be as subjective and pietistic as prayer and testimony. The melodies used are deeply rooted in the traditions of American gospel music. They are in themselves beautiful and edifying, but they take some getting used to for those persons from different cultural backgrounds.

It is only in the last generation—and, on the popular level, only in the last few years—that pentecostal people from the classical denominations have had much appreciation for higher education. In their culture there is not only a lack of interest in the intellectual life and in its contribution to the body of Christ, but there is also outright suspicion of study and research, especially in the areas of Scripture, theology, and related fields. There is rather a cultivation of religious, social, and political fundamentalism among the pentecostal people. This type of simplicity is encouraged and nourished in a milieu which sees ultimate questions answered primarily in terms of personal subjective experiences. These experiences are taken to be the work and witness of the Holy Spirit in one's soul; therefore value judgments are made almost entirely on the basis of personal experiences which are rather uncritically accepted as the movement, inspiration, and urging of the Holy Spirit.

There is a strong tendency among classical pentecostal people to accept their entire culture, their way of speaking, thinking, and praying, as well as their own personal thoughts and conclusions which proceed from themselves as individuals, as the leading of the Lord and the will of the Lord for them. This results in a considerable confusion between what is essential to the work and function of the Holy Spirit in their lives as individuals, and among them as congregations, and the culture in which this work of the Holy Spirit has been experienced. Indeed, while a distinction is made between the two, it is often thought that the culture is so intertwined with the work of the Holy Spirit that it would be a mistake to separate them from each other.

Let me quote here from an article by Kilian McDonnell, "Problems in Evaluating Catholic Pentecostalism" (*Dialogue*, Winter 1970): "One of the greatest obstacles to an impartial inquiry is the presence in neopentecostalism, both Catholic and Protestant, of what can be called cultural baggage. There is a classical pentecostal subculture or contraculture, which includes speech patterns, prayer postures, mental processes, expectation. This culture belongs to a specific historical, socio-cultural context, where it has its own validity. The classical pentecostal culture is not necessarily lower than other religious cultures but it is decidedly different. Neopentecostals very frequently forget that cultural baggage which has validity in one cultural context does not have validity in another. Cultural baggage is not transferable, and when the attempt is made to transfer the cultural baggage of classical pentecostalism to a Catholic context, then the problems become enormous. This usually means that the Catholic pentecostal is alienated from his Catholic brethren and is no longer able to operate effectively in a Roman Catholic community. The Catholic pentecostal thinks that he is being rejected for his pentecostalism; his Catholic friends think they are rejecting the phenomenon of pentecostalism while in fact they may only be rejecting the cultural baggage of classical pentecostalism. Baggage must not be understood here in the pejorative sense. It simply means the accouterments with which one passes through time. Baggage is culturally determined and is non-transferable. The pentecostal experience can be both profound and transforming. For the

Roman Catholic it can be such a revelation that the person receiving it makes no distinction between the central pentecostal reality, which is valid, and the cultural baggage, which is valid for classical pentecostals but not for others. Roman Catholics and Protestant neo-pentecostals who take over the cultural baggage place a great stumbling block to others in their own communions as they try to evaluate the pentecostal reality. For those who wish to embrace the pentecostal spirituality it is imperative that they remain true to their cultural traditions. Their task should be to integrate their pentecostal spirituality into their Catholic experience."

Classical pentecostals are not unaware of this concern and problem. In an interview to Fr. McDonnell by David DuPlessis in Copenhagen in 1968, DuPlessis gave this advice to neo-pentecostals: "Do not conform to pentecostal patterns, for example, clapping one's hands out of imitation of the [classical] pentecostals, or raising one's arms in prayer." In fact he has made an even stronger statement in his book *The Spirit Bade Me Go*: "Let me say right here that I consider it heresy to speak of shaking, trembling, falling, dancing, clapping, shouting, and such actions as manifestations of the Holy Spirit." Donald Gee, whose writings are accepted widely throughout classical pentecostalism, wrote in 1960: "It is a privilege to publish in this review thrilling stories of some recent 'pentecosts' in older denominational Churches. But let none deceive themselves. In the enthusiasm of their new experience these friends are likely to fall into just the same errors of fanaticism that we ourselves were guilty of forty or fifty years ago."

The Church has faced the problem of cultural transference over and over again in her history. At the very beginning of the New Testament Church the disciples of Christ were faced with the problem of whether they should continue to preach the Gospel in the Jewish context; they asked themselves whether Gentile converts to

Christianity were to be required to conform to Jewish cultural religious patterns of prayer and behavior. The answer given by the Holy Spirit in the first Council of Jerusalem, recorded in Acts 15, was decidedly in the negative. And so, the Church embarked upon a program lasting several hundred years which is commonly referred to as Hellenization: the translation of the authentic and essential message of the Gospel, the proclamation of the paschal mystery of our Lord and Savior Jesus Christ, in language and in cultural patterns intelligible to and humanly acceptable in the Greco-Roman world. In great measure, the conversion of the ancient world to Jesus Christ was due to this process of cultural adaptation.

The same problem confronted Christianity in the 16th century when the Church found herself on the threshold of great missionary ventures to the New World and the Far East. Among many missionaries there was a strong tendency, which has lasted in some quarters down to our day, to preach a European form of Christianity in the highly developed cultures of Japan and China. Some missionaries spent their entire lives learning the language, culture, thought patterns, modes of behavior, literature and art of the people to whom they were sent. Thus they were able to find ways of communicating the authentic and pure Gospel of Jesus Christ in a way in which it could be appropriated by the people of the strange culture. On the other hand there were those who insisted on exporting Portuguese Christianity or Spanish Christianity to the Far East. They walked into a completely different cultural situation and preached in a manner that was understood in the lands from which they came but which was incomprehensible in the lands to which they went. Therefore their work bore little fruit, while the work of the former missionaries who had carefully adapted themselves to the culture they were speaking to bore, slowly and over a long period of time, good solid fruit in the emergence of dedicated Christian communities. The "Europeanizers" in the 16th century, as the "Judaizers" in the 1st century, confused the wonderful works of God in the salvation wrought for us in Jesus Christ with the culturally-bound manifestations and expressions of that event. Through this confusion the communication of the Gospel was impeded.

Catholics experiencing charismatic renewal in the Church today, and Protestant pentecostals anxious to contribute to it, are faced with precisely this same problem. While we must be extremely careful that what takes place under the name of charismatic renewal is to the best of our knowledge the authentic work of the Holy Spirit among us, and while we must remain radically open to the various ways in which the Lord may decide to move among us, we must also be extremely careful not to import into the Catholic charismatic movement those purely human elements which properly and rightly belong among classical pentecostals as part of their religious and cultural traditions. These elements frequently have no place in the Catholic theological, spiritual, and cultural tradition, and they have little resonance with contemporary American Catholicism.

This does not mean that Catholics should not pray spontaneously or with hands outstretched or upraised. Nor am I suggesting that we must retain a kind of somberness or stiffness in our prayer meetings. Our music should be a genuine reflection of the wonders the Lord is doing among us, as should be our testimony, our teaching and our preaching. But let the form of these elements of our spiritual life come authentically from us as the people we are. Let these forms grow organically from our own cultural background so that they will be authentically part of our total lives and not just in the "pentecostal corner" of our lives, so that our corporate witness may be more relevant to and meaningful to the vast majority of present-day Catholics. Let us not import the cultural expressions of a group of people so different on the natural level from ourselves, either out of a desire to imitate them or to become like them, or because we love them and are grateful to them for everything they have done for us.

On the other hand, let no one criticize or ridicule pentecostal culture among the classical pentecostal people. Let us nurture a genuine respect for the way the Lord has worked among them and for the type of people they are. Let us lovingly accept them as brothers and sisters in Christ. Let us see deeply beyond the cultural differences that may in some sense separate us; and let us love each other on that deeper level so much that when we are at one of their meetings we may experience the freedom to enter into the life of the Spirit as it is being manifested there with perfect freedom and authenticity. Reciprocally they, in coming to our meetings, will be able to be comfortable and to participate with respect for our way of doing things.

Dogmatic Differences

The question of mutual respect can also pass into those areas of difference which might be termed dogmatic. The doctrinal differences which still separate Catholic and denominational pentecostal Christians are many and complex. Certainly this is an area of study and concern deserving of intense research and thorough treatment. Already there are signs that competent theologians representing Catholic and Protestant pentecostal points of view are preparing to undertake ecumenical dialogue in good faith and with serious purpose. Certainly we cannot hope here adequately to present or reflect upon the many serious differences in faith which still exist between brothers and sisters under the lordship of Jesus Christ.

Nevertheless we cannot leave the subject of Catholic-Protestant pentecostal relationships without at least attempting to structure some of the problems which we know exist and which we continually encounter in our relationships with each other.

Knowledge of some attitudes and beliefs on both sides of the issues may be of assistance when questions of a doctrinal nature arise in the normal course of our fellowship. There is a serious temptation, which I think all of us experience, to plunge ahead into amateur theological discussions with each other across denominational lines, anxious perhaps to share or to convince another of the authenticity and correctness of one's own point of view. It is my opinion that such types of dialogue should be approached cautiously and only with adequate preparation and under competent direction. By and large, the issues which divide us dogmatically are far too complex even to be stated clearly in any sort of brief discussion. They are questions which carry with them the weight and suffering of the Reformation and Counter Reformation in the history of Western Christianity. They must be approached responsibly and, I believe, corporately, with genuine respect for each other and with mutual desire only for the ultimate upbuilding of the body of Christ.

We must not only respect each other in this, but respect the action of the Holy Spirit among us in these days. He will guide our steps. But at this time, while cultivating openness and understanding to each other's perspectives, any attitude except loyalty and adherence to our own different theological traditions and beliefs would not only be premature but a serious error. Increased understanding of the basic differences in points of view may serve as a guideline to us for understanding each other and for protecting the "unity of the Spirit in the bond of peace" which the Lord has so graciously been building up in the last four years.

We note, for example, a certain difference in our approach to and attitude toward Sacred Scripture which both pentecostals and Catholics accept unequivocally to be the inspired Word of God. However the pentecostals, as all Protestant fundamentalists, regard the Bible as the sole inspired infallible teaching of God, applicable directly and literally to every phase of Christian belief and behavior. Everything is to be known and decided on the basis of this written Word, and by that is meant, it seems to me, on what the written expression of the Word of God says verbally, word by word, paragraph by paragraph. There is perhaps a tendency to regard the "literal" sense of Scripture as what it says plainly and simply in English translation. Consequently, there is grave hesitation to arrive at a deeper understanding of the literal sense of Scripture through exegesis and through the resonances of the Word proclaimed throughout the body of Christ. In its *Decree of Ecumenism* Vatican Council II notes with considerable enthusiasm the devotion and adherence of our separated brethren to the Sacred Scriptures, but it also notes that here we find something of a cult of the Bible itself (n. 21).

Perhaps it might be expressed in this way: From personal observation it seems to me that for most fundamentalists the Bible, as the sole rule, is set up as the instrument of God over, above, and separated from the Church herself. Scripture seems to stand outside the Church, so to speak (although it is surely proclaimed within the Church), and, standing outside the Church, it gives direction to the Church.

The Catholic point of view is considerably different. There is no question that the Bible is affirmed to be the inspired Word of God. As it has been given by the Holy Spirit to the people of God throughout salvation history, it is a testimony to the authentic faith and a primary source of spiritual direction and nourishment. Scripture, however, from a Catholic point of view stands at the heart of, or as the core of, the whole Christian tradition. It stands very much *within* the Church; it was inspired and written within the Church, is proclaimed in the Church, reverberates throughout the Church and through her various members according to their different functions, and it is applied to the body of Christ as it is interpreted in that living organism.

From these different points of view flow a multitude of differences which not only separate Catholics and pentecostals, but are the meat and matter of most ecumenical dialogue going on today. We must note, however, that from the conservative Protestant point of view it is difficult for the pentecostal to understand or to justify any practice or belief in the life of the Church or of the individual believer which is not explicitly and word for word laid out in Scripture. To the Catholic mind, since it is believed that the inspiration of the Holy Spirit is operative in the life of the Church as a whole as well as in Scripture (which is nevertheless uniquely inspired), the Holy Spirit acts authentically in a variety of ways: in teaching, in sacramental celebration, in prayer, and in the ordinary life of the Catholic people.

Other Areas of Disagreement

We can also note other major differences. Due to the historical roots traceable from early Methodism and the holiness movement, Protestant pentecostalism in its pastoral theology tends to focus on certain crisis experiences taking place during Christian life which are believed to be the absolute and definitive events in the life of the believer—events which radically change the believer's relationship to God as the result of an individual faith commitment. The crisis experience of salvation or conversion, as well as (for some persons) a crisis experience of sanctification, and in all cases a crisis experience of baptism in the Holy Spirit, mark for the pentecostal *the* events in one's personal Christian life. They tend to be the focus of all teaching, preaching and pastoral care. One's life in Christ is dated and related in terms of these experiences, which are normally expressed as individual encounters between the Lord and one particular believer.

In contrast, we note that Catholic spirituality is to a considerable degree more communal, based on and rooted in the sacramental celebration of the liturgy, in and through which the risen Lord by the power of his Holy Spirit acts upon and in his mystical body at once corporately and personally. Life in Christ, from a Catholic point of view, is genuinely begun in baptism where we are born again of water and the Spirit. It continues to grow and develop as a process under the impulse of the Holy Spirit. Quite definitely there is much room in Catholic spirituality for definite personal experiences such as conversion or baptism in the Holy Spirit. It is because of the authenticity of such experiences in the Catholic tradition that the present relationship between Catholic and Protestant pentecostals is taking place.

Another area of principal concern in our relationship is that the pentecostal fundamentalist, using the Bible as he has been taught to use and understand it, cannot find justification for Catholic doctrine and practice in regard to the celebration of the eucharist with its theology of transubstantiation, sacrifice, and priesthood; nor can he fully accept the sacraments of penance and baptism, the role of Mary and the saints in the economy of salvation, and the function of the papacy. I list these particular issues simply on the basis of the frequency with which they have been raised to me. I hear them over and over again whenever I go to predominantly Protestant pentecostal assemblies to present the testimony of what the Lord has done for us. As I said above, the Protestant pentecostal does not find for these practices any scriptural warrant that he regards as satisfactory. He does not allow the principle of the development of doctrine and practice under the guidance of the Holy Spirit in the body of Christ in the same way that the Catholic Church understands it to be operating.

Furthermore, the Protestant pentecostal understanding of these Catholic doctrines tends to be a distortion or caricature of what the authentic Catholic teaching really is. In the welter of post-Reformation rhetoric, both sides have become accustomed to examining each other through fogged-up glasses.

In terms of these areas of disagreement, I think we must note an attitude and then a principle. The attitude of our Protestant pentecostal brethren seems to be this: Since you have been converted to Christ and have been baptized in the Holy Spirit, surely now you will come into the "fullness of the truth," or at least the basic truths which the Holy Spirit has been teaching us (pentecostals) all along. "Truth" here would mean the understanding of dogmatics along basically conservative fundamental lines which differ considerably from the dogmatic position of the Catholic Church on a number of points. This attitude just described varies from individual to individual. The vast majority of Protestant pentecostals of my acquaintance are interested and genuinely concerned with our spiritual well-being. Believing themselves in possession of the truth, they are anxious for us to share in it, and they raise these questions out of good will, love, and concern for us. I think we must appreciate that. A much smaller, yet consistently vocal, number of people seem primarily interested in achieving a renunciation of our Catholic belief coupled with a new adherence to fundamental Protestant dogmatics. When that is not forthcoming, this small group then begins to question the validity of our experience. For, they say, if the experience were genuine the Holy Spirit would have led us to "the truth."

Here we come to a principle which I think applies to these attitudes. We read in the gospel of John: "When the Spirit of truth comes, he will guide you into all the truth" (Jn. 16, 13). It is extremely important, particularly since this verse is used consistently by our Protestant pentecostal brethren in regard to these matters, to note that, as far as they are concerned, this verse means: "When the Holy Spirit has come to you personally—i.e., when you have been baptized in the Holy Spirit individually and personally—then the Holy Spirit, who is the Spirit of truth, will lead you personally and individually to the fullness of truth." Arriving at "all the truth" is taken to be something of an evidence of the authenticity of the experience of the baptism in the Holy Spirit.

The same sort of principle is applied by a number of other fundamentalists, who are not of pentecostal persuasion, to the action of the Holy Spirit consequent to a personal conversion. I think it safe to say that the general Catholic reaction to this proposition is that the promise made by Jesus to those who were with him at the Last Supper—that when the Spirit came he would lead them into all truth—was a promise made to the whole Church corporately, and rather specifically through a function of the teaching office in the Church. In the very context of the statement, it is said to a group, not to an individual. It has been consistently interpreted in the Church as a promise made to the Church in her entirety, and to be realized in the Church through various ministries of authoritative teaching.

Some Suggestions

It seems to me that the basic responsibility of Catholics involved in the charismatic renewal, in terms of doctrinal differences with Protestant pentecostals, can be spelled out in several steps. First of all we must recognize that the baptism in the Holy Spirit has led us to deeper Christian faith as members of the Roman Catholic Church. For us it is a general characteristic of the baptism in the Holy Spirit that it increases our faith in the

Roman Church and in her authentic teaching and practice as the unique and intense manifestation of the body of Christ that she is. As through the Spirit we have become more loyal to Christ, so we have become more loyal to the Church and her teaching, since we see her as a Spirit-led instrument of Christ in the world.

Loyalty, however, is not enough. Because of our increased desire to witness to the truth of the Gospel, and because of our new relationships with Christians of other denominations, we have a strong obligation to study carefully and to learn the authentic teaching of the Church on a wide variety of dogmatic subjects, and to seek under the guidance of the Holy Spirit, together with the best teaching and counseling that is available, an ever better understanding of the truths of the faith.

At the same time, in spite of our differences, we need to cultivate an intense respect for the beliefs that our brothers and sisters have. Respect for them, love for them, desire to share life in Christ and the Spirit with them —all this does not mean that we will all agree on every point in Christian dogma. We need to respect them and the way the Lord has been working through them, just as we have, in fact, experienced that they respect us and our beliefs because they respect the way the Lord has been working among us. It seems to me that only such mutual respect and openness, even in the face of confusion and our own inability to understand the ways of God, is a sure sign of our acceptance of the freedom of the Holy Spirit working among all the Christian people today.

We must be careful that we do not jump to the conclusion that simply because our Protestant pentecostal brethren have been blessed by the Lord with the very wonderful experience of the baptism in the Holy Spirit, and perhaps through their ministry we have been blessed with the same experience, we must now automatically adopt their understanding of Scripture and dogma. To do so would be to confuse and equate the gracious action of God in this outpouring of the Holy Spirit with certain people's understanding of its meaning and significance.

On the other hand, we must remain open to the forms of faith expression used by our brothers. We must not preemptively dismiss anything they say or teach simply because it sounds foreign to our ears. Time and time again in the last four years, the teaching of Protestant pentecostals, while couched in an often strange vocabulary, has served to enliven and build up aspects of our Christian life while being totally in harmony with Catholic teaching.

It is equally true that this process of edification has been operating in the other direction as well. Protestant pentecostals have been, and are, in the process of learning a great deal about the richness of full Christian life from the Catholic witness in areas such as the celebration of the liturgy, traditional methods of prayer and the spiritual life, and the implications of the Gospel for Christian social responsibility.

The oneness in the Spirit which the Lord has created among Catholics and Protestants through the baptism in the Spirit is a precious miracle of grace in our day. I do not believe we have begun to grasp the significance of this breakthrough in the unfolding of God's plan for his people. The sharing of a faith common to us all, the growth in mutual trust and understanding in areas of cultural and doctrinal differences, the growing ability to pray and worship together genuinely while maintaining our integrity—all this is creating a new, strong, bold, witness to the reality and saving power of the Gospel of Jesus Christ. I believe that as this unity is preserved and deepened in honesty and love, we shall see the Spirit-driven Word proclaimed and lived out with remarkable success for the upbuilding of the kingdom.

Life in Community

Ralph Martin

From the New Testament it is clear that God's gift of his Spirit to those who embrace the saving death and resurrection of his Son, Jesus, is intended to effect an experiential reconciliation not only between God and man, but also between man and man. It is also clear that the reconciliation between men is intended not only to produce a change of heart, a bringing about of forgiveness and universal love, but also to issue forth and become visible in a new style of life—Christian community life.

It is essential to God's plan and desire that those who embrace the saving work of his Son and receive his Spirit yield to the impulse of that Spirit to make them visibly one. In those passages of St. John's gospel with which we have become so familiar, where the great promises of Jesus to send the Spirit are related, we find expressed the fervent desire of Jesus that his followers yield to the will of the Father and the Spirit that they become one—visibly one—so that the world may come to faith. "I do not pray for these only, but also for those who believe in me through their word, that they may all be one; even as you, Father, are in me, and I in you, that they also may be in us, so that the world may believe that you have sent me. The glory which you have given me I have given to them, that they may be one even as we are one, I in them and you in me, that they may become

145

perfectly one so that the world may know that you have sent me and have loved them even as you have loved me" (Jn. 17, 20–23).

It is an essential part of God's plan, then, that those who follow his Son and receive his Spirit enter into a life of union and love with God and one another so that the Gospel may be believed and men may believe in Jesus and enter into the salvation that they perceive and experience in the Christian community. *Christianity is essentially communal, and yielding to God must mean yielding to a community form of life.*

Those who have been experiencing the pouring out of God's Spirit in the charismatic renewal have been coming to realize more and more the essential link between receiving the Holy Spirit and yielding to a community form of life. Just a few years ago, at the beginning of the renewal, we tended to see the baptism in the Holy Spirit mainly as an individual experience. Our experience and thought over the past few years have brought us to the awareness that this is but an introduction to a life in the Spirit in community. Previously, we sought to understand the place and purpose of the charismatic gifts by exploring them individually; we now see more and more that they are essentially linked to a life in community. It is interesting in this regard to notice that when Paul speaks at length concerning the charismatic gifts, he also introduces, for the first time in the New Testament, a very full description of the communal nature of our Christianity in terms of our being members of one body. "For just as the body is one and has many members, and all the members of the body, though many, are one body, so it is with Christ. For by one Spirit we were all baptized into one body. . . . For the body does not consist of one member but of many. . . . Now you are the body of Christ and individually members of it" (1 Cor. 12, 12–27). The charismatic gifts then, are given and exercised to build up—to bring to a greater development, unity and harmony—the body of Christians. Most of them require a community context to be exercised meaningfully, and all of them have as their purpose to bring to a deeper level that communal life union between God and man, and between man and man.

In fact I would go so far as to say that someone who is not in a regular and committed community contact with other Christians is not in a situation where God can make him into what he most desires him to be, is not where God wants him to be. I would also say that where there are serious Christians living in a situation where there is no possibility of community contact, they ought to seriously consider whether God wants them to move or not. This obviously will not always be the right thing to do, but it does express the seriousness with which God wants us to regard his desire to build us into a community. This desire is of the essence of the new covenant.

Moreover, over the past few years we have begun to look beyond (while not neglecting) the great and revolutionary truths and realities concerning the charismatic experience itself. We are looking to the effects of that experience in life, especially in the development of community. After the first Pentecost, one of the most notable effects of the Spirit was the growth and development of a communal form of life of early believers which seemed to have the evangelistic results Jesus had indicated: "And all who believed were together and had all things in common; and they sold their possessions and goods and distributed them to all, as any had need. And day by day, attending the temple together and breaking bread in their homes, they partook of food with glad and generous hearts, praising God and having favor with all the people. And the Lord added to their number day by day those who were being saved" (Acts 2, 44–47).

Increasingly it is becoming clearer from experience as well as from Scripture that the baptism in the Spirit cannot bear the fruit it promises unless it indeed serves

as a gateway to a life lived increasingly in community.
The baptism in the Spirit can no longer be looked upon
as an isolated religious experience; rather, it is the releas-
ing of the power of the Spirit to build us into a living
community in which the knowledge and experience of
God can increase and grow, and in which men and women
can be attracted daily to the life of the Lord as manifested
in his body, his temple, his Church, his people, his community.

The Need for Leadership

Already in the short history of the charismatic renewal in the Catholic Church, a failure in some areas,
and among some people, to comprehend and act on the
essential link between receiving the Holy Spirit and living a life in community has caused a number of unfortu-
nate situations to develop. In one city which was very
prominent in the first year or two of the present outpouring, hundreds of Catholics were baptized in the
Spirit, and the city gained a national reputation as a
center of the Catholic charismatic renewal. Now, a few
years later, a small group of Catholics are struggling to
begin again to hold prayer meetings and share what God
is doing with others in the area. Out of the hundreds
originally involved, only a few have persevered in seeking to live and enter more deeply into a life lived in the
Spirit. Many—after the initial enthusiasm was over and
nothing much came of their experience—became hostile
and bitter concerning any efforts to interest them in attempting to live in the Spirit. More is needed than simply
turning people on, laying on hands, and praising the
Lord if the baptism in the Spirit is to be more than an
isolated experience.

But this is not a phenomenon unique to Catholics
involved in the charismatic renewal. Over the past ten

years other churches which have become involved with it have experienced similar things. One Episcopalian lay leader, very active in the renewal, related recently how, over the past several years, hundreds of Episcopalians in a particular area of California were baptized in the Spirit; but today it is hard to find any trace of this. They have disappeared into the woodwork. Our Episcopalian friend also said, from what he has seen happening among Catholics in certain areas of the country, that we may escape this disappointment because we have discovered and accepted two essential things: (1) that we must not despise or neglect to use needed human leadership, and (2) that we must lay strong emphasis on the necessary link between receiving the Spirit and living a community life. This chapter attempts only to explore these and some of the other factors that a number of Catholic communities have found to be true as regards the practical decisions and principles which affect the development of a solid Christian community.

In many manifestations of the charismatic renewal there exists what must simply be called a prejudice against human leadership. And understandably so. The outpouring of the Spirit is a breath of fresh air in a Church which has been closed in many ways to the here-and-now direct workings of the Spirit, a Church which has generated project after project, a Church which is properly seen as a work of the flesh or of the human will and mind rather than of the Spirit of God. It is true, and it must be said, that what is of the flesh is flesh, and what is of the Spirit is Spirit. And only what is of the Spirit will give life.

The way in which leadership is exercised in the Church frequently indicates a lack of awareness of the desire of the Spirit to reveal, to give guidance, to lead, to witness, etc. It is understandable and desirable that in the charismatic renewal we need to remain optimally open to the full working of the Lord—indeed, if you will, to the sovereign moving of the Lord. Yet in the plan of God the active cooperation of human beings has always been important for allowing him to carry out his work. Total docility to the Holy Spirit doesn't usually lead to total passivity, but rather to Spirit-inspired activity. The Lord invited Peter to come to him over the water. It was necessary for Peter to respond and cooperate with his human faculties by standing up in the boat, stepping over the gunwale and beginning to walk. God's part was to sustain him as he walked. But Peter had to walk, to move forward, for God's power to come into play. With God's plan to build up a body, it is the same situation. There is a need for human response and cooperation with his invitation to become a people, to become one. Paul describes God's desire for unity and growth in his people and the means which he will offer to effect this end. He describes certain gifts of human beings who will be able to perform important services for the body to grow: "And his gifts were that some should be apostles, some prophets, some evangelists, some pastors and teachers, for the equipment of the saints, the work of ministry, for building up the body of Christ, until we all attain to the unity of the faith and of the knowledge of the Son of God, to mature manhood, to the measure of the stature of the fullness of Christ; so that we may no longer be children. . . . Rather, speaking the truth in love, we are to grow up in every way into him who is the head, into Christ, from whom the whole body, joined and knit together by every joint with which it is supplied, when each part is working properly, makes bodily growth and upbuilds itself in love" (Eph. 4, 11–16).

These ministry gifts take years to develop to maturity. A person newly baptized in the Spirit-community would not be likely to possess these ministries in anything like mature form. Most communities may find it useful initially to depend on ministries supplied from more mature communities or from itinerant Catholic "ministers" who make them available in a wider way by traveling. These ministries are not the only important services in the community, but they are the ones which allow the others to come into being and to develop as they should. It is the function first of the apostle and then of the pastor to take as his responsibility the job of seeing to it that all the gifts operate in the body as the Spirit wills. It is the function of the apostle (the one or ones bringing a new community into being) and then of the pastor (who assumes the overall responsibility when the apostle moves on) to take overall responsibility for the development of the community, for its health and unity. Those who might have the seeds of pastoral responsibility should begin to gather together to pray, to think, to discuss and to take action for the overall development of the community. This function simply must be exercised if a community is to exist at all. If thinking about community formation in terms of those who have the seeds of a pastoral or apostolic ministry seems threatening or forbidding, another way of viewing it is the gathering together of those who might be developing into "elders" of the community, those of some maturity and stability and experience who can serve as the "older brothers" of the community in real pastoral concern and care.

In those areas of the country where small groups of men and women have begun to gather together to take responsibility for what is happening and to discern what God might want to do and what their cooperation ought to be, things have begun to happen. In areas where no one has assumed this responsibility and pastoral leadership, nothing much has happened, and often the charismatic renewal has ended up being only a flash in the pan.

Three Patterns of Life

In the charismatic renewal there are many different ways in which people associate with one another, and a wide range of purposes. Some come together "when the Spirit moves them" or when they feel like it for purposes of fellowship, support, and sharing, without going much beyond this. There are cities where the normal pattern of life involves contact at certain big events, monthly meetings, etc. There are individuals for whom the normal pattern involves dropping in on prayer meetings when they feel like it, perhaps going to different ones as they feel led. Quite another pattern that has developed is that of the regular weekly prayer meeting which is attended faithfully by a number of persons and which is also a host to newcomers and "floaters."

The third pattern which seems to be developing in some places of the country is that of groups of people who are led to commit themselves to one another and to the Lord to allow him to build them into a full body of Christ with all the gifts, functions, and services that the Lord desires to exist in each "local church." Their association is more, therefore, than just casual or weekly prayer meetings; it has been broadened to include various degrees of living together. Whether it means living in the same household or apartment building, or living closer to one another in some other way, by having meals together or being together in prayer, study, and action during the week, intimate relationships start to form. The first pattern of conduct could perhaps be described as "fellowship"; the latter can be described as a "covenant" relationship. Different people in different situations will be led to different forms of association. But one thing that is becoming increasingly clear is that only when there is a fully functioning "local church" after the pattern of the New Testament churches do the same things that happen in the New Testament happen consistently today. There seems to be a dynamic intrinsic to the life in the Spirit which leads these prayer groups to develop into full communities. For the Spirit to fully express himself in bringing out the life of Jesus, we sense a need to have a real community where there is a closeness, intimacy, unity and commitment. Only in this way does it seem possible for the full purposes of God to be accomplished—in the growth of his disciples and in the spread of his Gospel. A hasty or premature decision to "create community" is a real danger, but to ignore the need to weigh before the Lord the kind of commitment he is calling the leaders and community to make would most likely grieve the Spirit. No matter how the Lord may seek to develop a particular group of people, nothing much happens until there are at least a few people in the area who make a significant commitment to one another and the Lord, making themselves unlimitedly available to him and his purposes.

Charismatic and "Mixed" Groups

Another decision that has to be made (or it will be made by default) is whether the community will be "mixed" (some receiving and believing in the baptism in the Spirit and charismatic gifts, including tongues, and some not so inclined) or "completely" charismatic. A common phenomenon is for a community to begin with a group of people experiencing the baptism in the Spirit, with some at least speaking in tongues; they start having prayer meetings which new people come to. Gradually they begin to accept a situation where some of the "regulars" in the community have asked for the baptism in the Spirit, while others haven't asked and don't intend to, but they want to be part of the group for sharing prayer or some kind of friendship. What usually happens in such prayer meetings, then, is that people participate in them with one eye on the Lord and one eye on each other, with the consequent effect of strongly inhibiting the freedom and responsiveness of those open to all the operations of the Spirit. Praying or speaking in tongues, free and expressive praise, and all other activities will be inhibited. There will be a subtle but strong pressure to "level off" the prayer meeting as a prayer-share group, steering away from the more manifest or direct manifestations of the Spirit. Subtly a whole set of limitations on what can be talked about or in what way the baptism of the Spirit can be spoken of will be set up. I personally believe that making an accommodation like this will effectively block the significant working of God's Spirit. From the start it is important for those interested in an openly charismatic "full Gospel" community to make it clear that that is the basis on which the group gets together. Those who are not comfortable with a group like this would be better off joining any of the wide number of prayer-share groups that abound in today's Church rather than deactiviating the charismatic openness of the group. The "full Gospel" should be preached and lived in such a way that it would be impossible for a sizable number of people to continue to come without choosing for or against receiving the baptism of the Spirit and the manifestations which follow. If a group doesn't decide to be unabashedly "pentecostal," it gets so tied up in accommodations to one person's fear or another person's doubt that it never gets anywhere. Prayer meetings should not be "put on" for newcomers; however, all persons should be allowed to come to see and experience "full Gospel" Christians praising their God. Indeed, only when people are free in the Spirit before the Lord will the Spirit be able to work to bring newcomers to a deep fear of the Lord, which is the true beginning of wisdom and conversion.

In a way, all the fundamental decisions flow from

whether or not a group has asserted its willingness and eagerness to go "all the way" with the Lord and whether or not it has taken away all restrictions it may be tempted to place on how the Lord may work. And there is a strong tendency among Catholic charismatic groups to place a rather low ceiling on what the Lord can do. Some, when they ask for the baptism in the Spirit, are asking for just a little more of the Spirit, not too much; and that's what they get. Some are willing to change their lives to a certain degree, but not to "go to extremes." Only in those individuals and groups that are willing to abandon themselves completely to the Lord, and who with no restrictions are willing to leave all things for his sake, can God truly accomplish his purposes in the world. Whether to let go completely in every conceivable way is the basic decision facing those involved in charismatic renewal.

Preparing for Community Life

As mentioned before, it seems as if there is an internal dynamic to the activity of the Spirit which impels people toward a close, unlimited community. And nowhere does that become more apparent than when we try to understand how to help people to be baptized in the Spirit. In fact, the more experience we have in trying to help people in this way, the more our fundamental concept of what's happening changes; it becomes no longer a task of helping people to be baptized in the Spirit, but helping them to live in a deeper way their life in the Spirit in community. The two have become fully intertwined. It becomes then a matter of adding new people to a definitely existing constituted community. As Luke reports in Acts, "And the Lord added to their number, day by day, those who were being saved." There was a definite community to which the Lord added people, and they thus became part of the life of that definite community. Being "saved," receiving the Spirit, meant becoming a definite part of a quite definite community.

When we were first praying with people for the baptism in the Spirit in Ann Arbor, we began to realize that some kind of preparation for people before praying with them might be in order. This usually involved some kind of explanation, at first informal, and then formal, of what the baptism in the Spirit was. We began to see people who had not, and who were not, prepared to commit their lives to Christ and yet who were nonetheless seeking the baptism in the Spirit. That was impossible, and the realization was disconcerting. So we began to stress the acceptance of Christ more centrally, no longer presupposing that somehow it mysteriously got communicated when talking about the baptism in the Spirit. After a while, in evaluating the results, we noticed that of all the people who really met Christ and received the baptism in the Spirit, those who then made close friendships in the group with those who were committed most strongly, tended to persevere and grow, no matter what their initial experience was. After a time they began to steady out into a genuine and growing life in the Spirit. This led us to re-evaluate our understanding of community. Over the past few years we've drawn steadily nearer to a satisfactory way of helping people into a solid life in the Spirit, one which has passed from simple preparation, to preparation plus follow-up, to an integrated process of new people being added to the community. As one of the steps of the process they received the baptism of the Spirit. We're still groping toward a vision the Spirit has given us, a glimpse which looks more and more like the catechumenate of the early Church.

In an open, public prayer meeting once a week, a variety of ways are provided for people to come to understand the experience of a community living in the

Spirit. There is a formal explanation session before and after the meeting, an available supply of literature displayed, and people who take a special responsibility in greeting newcomers. Those who are desirous of entering into a deeper life in the Spirit (one phase of which would be praying for the baptism in the Spirit) are invited each week to come to the Life in the Spirit Seminars which take place each week an hour before the meeting begins, at a specified location in the same building. Those who come in a given week are invited to remain together as a group and go through the six sessions together, under the guidance of a two-man team who will remain with the group for the whole six weeks. By having the same group stay together for six weeks with the same two team members, an actual community is in fact formed, and over the course of the six weeks they become built into the community. There's also a chance for each person to open up to the Lord at his own pace. Also in this way the "baptism in the Spirit" doesn't stick out as an isolated religious experience, which a person "gets" and then does as he pleases. It is simply one of the things involved in entering into a stable and growing life in the Spirit in community. Teaching and sharing on growth and community are woven into the whole process. The Lord has been able to work very powerfully and deeply through these means, and we look forward to even further growth. There is considerably more to solid community growth than simply praying with people for the baptism in the Spirit; there is a world to be discovered, and principles and laws of spiritual and community growth to be revealed, if a true body of Christ is to mature and develop.

The Structure of a Community

In many places in the Church today "structure" is an unpopular concept. There is no doubt that much of today's structure is not facilitating life in the Spirit but hindering it. But for anyone who has had practical experience with living Christian communities, it is not a question of structure or no structure; it is a question of which structures are conducive or not conducive to facilitate a deeper life in the Spirit at this stage of development. No building or temple can be built unless there is scaffolding and framework to allow building materials to form. No life exists without some structure. In the human body, which Paul says is analogous to the life of reborn Christians, it is the skeleton which allows life to take shape and form, providing a support for life to form. Because the Christian community is a living body, an organism, it needs structure. Because it is a growing organism, it needs an evolving, developing structure. What is suitable to facilitate life and shape at a particular stage of development may deaden life at a later stage. One of the main concerns of those with pastoral responsibility is to discern what structure is needed at what time. If this is neglected or left to chance, an unhealthy or misshapen body, or none at all, will result. Discerning how God is moving, how the body is growing, and the structure (procedures, policies, forms) needed to support that life is one of the chief pastoral responsibilities.

A common structural question run into by many communities is the question of what to do when the community grows beyond the point when everybody knows everybody on the level of personal friendship. A natural tendency is to think about splitting into smaller prayer groups or communities. In at least some situations it seems advisable not to split the meeting or community, but to encourage the formation of smaller groups on formal and informal bases (formal Bible studies, as well as informal gatherings for prayer, dinner, visiting, etc.), and to keep the community together in one unified meeting once a week.

The advantages of this are several. For one thing it

seems as though many smaller groups don't quite have the same evangelistic impact as the witness of one large group praising the Lord in the power of the Spirit. The sight of 100 or 400 people praising the Lord has a powerful impact on newcomers, which seldom happens in a small home group. Also, it seems that splitting up without maintaining a unified meeting contact sometimes divides the resources so that there is not enough mature leadership in each group to really help it to develop. Mature leadership takes a long time to develop. True apostles, prophets, evangelists, teachers and pastors within a group aren't so plentiful in any city to guarantee that each small group will end up with the resources it needs to grow. A certain pooling of resources in a central prayer meeting seems advisable in many situations at an early stage of growth.

Those who have more developed gifts of preaching, leading prophecy, etc., are able to feed the whole body in a particular area. The saying "In numbers there is strength" seems to hold true in many ways in the initial stages of community development. Questions of geography, travel distance, etc., are relevant in discerning what structures are needed to support a maximum life in the Spirit in a community, and the natural tendency to split prematurely should be carefully prayed over, with the advantages of a unified community kept in mind.

A chapter of this length can do little more than survey the factors that are essential to the solid growth of Christian community. Each one of the factors is deserving of at least a chapter of its own, and in the years to come I expect that we will see a number of articles about them. For what we are involved in is not merely a discovery of the power of the Spirit, but a whole complex of pastoral theories and practices which went into the building and sustaining of Spirit-filled communities that for all practical purposes within Catholicism have been sorely neglected if not entirely lost. But would at least like to mention some other critical areas to which we must give our attention if our communities are going to grow strong in the Spirit. At the stage of development where many of us are, it is necessary to become aware of these areas to be explored further in prayer, study, and communication with each other if we are to move closer to the goal.

1. *Problem People:* Any community must soon face up to the fact that not all persons who have been attracted to the community are psychologically and spiritually mature. Indeed, serious psychological and spiritual immaturity, and even sickness, will almost certainly be present in some members. If this is ignored or brushed aside for fear of the responsibility involved in acknowledging such problems and the feeling of inadequacy in dealing with them, it could certainly and seriously block the development of the community—and even result in tragedy of one form or another. It is imperative that those with pastoral responsibility commit themselves to coming to grips with the existence of this area of need. Often people with problems will be those most eager to share, to give counsel to others, to exercise the spiritual gifts, all in an off-centered way. Learning how to speak the truth in love to one another and to those with more serious problems is imperative. To speak the truth without love is destructive, but to love without speaking the truth can be equally disastrous. If a way of helping these people is not immediately available (an experienced counselor, professional help, the healing gifts of the Spirit) in a mature enough form to be effective, then at the very minimum these people must be asked to refrain from ministering in any form until such help is available and has become effective in their lives.

2. *Protestant Involvement:* We who are Catholics owe an immense debt to our Protestant brothers who helped us to come into, experience, and understand the world of the charismatic workings of the Spirit. Many of

the significant forward steps and breakthroughs in the development of our community in Ann Arbor continue to come directly through contact with Protestant pentecostals. We have learned much from them, and there is much yet to learn. One disturbing development in some places is a certain Catholic arrogance that begrudgingly acknowledges some Protestant contribution in the past but supposes that "we" have things well in hand and can proceed ahead without them. The opposite attitude also appears in places, and is equally disturbing. Some, unaware of the workings of the Spirit in the Catholic tradition and also unaware of some of the most tragic weaknesses in Protestant pentecostalism, uncritically accept everything Protestant—from tenuous exegetical interpretations to unacceptable doctrinal practices. Discerning how the Spirit desires to work among us in this area is critically important. It requires much wisdom, humility and love, as well as strength in acting on what the Spirit says. While we have invited Protestants to come and minister to us, we also on occasion have had to invite them not to do so, when it appeared that they were insensitive to how the Spirit was working among us. While we know that what the Lord is doing has tremendous implications for the unity of Christians, we are cautious about becoming just another "interdenominational" charismatic group. We feel that the Lord is leading us to grow as a community which is open to all but Catholic at its core, and that he desires to use us primarily at the moment as a witness within the Catholic Church.

3. *New Wine and Old Wineskins:* The Gospel truth that new wine can't be contained in old wineskins is applicable to the present new outpouring of the Spirit. Many present structures and forms of the Catholic Church are not maximally conducive to a full life as a Spirit-filled community. Many parishes, dioceses, and religious orders present huge obstacles to living a full life

in the Spirit. What to do in situations like this requires great love, wisdom and tact. It is not yet clear how the Spirit is leading in the matter of relating the growing charismatic communities to the structures of parishes, dioceses and religious orders of which their members are also a part.

Everyone in the charismatic renewal will experience this tension. As we live more and more deeply a life in the Spirit in community, the more we will also experience a certain tension with life in the communities to which we have prior and serious commitments—those of our family, parish, diocese or religious order. Every age of renewal, though, has produced the same tensions—including, archetypically, the renewal that Jesus of Nazareth himself brought to the already existing religious situation of his day. The authentic solution in that day, and in centuries later during the monastic renewal, in the Franciscan renewal and in other renewals up to our time, has always been to live fully and deeply, to accept fully the new outpouring of graces that God is giving, resisting the temptation to close in on oneself, to become a sect or an un-Christian elite.

The solution to tension is not to deny or cut off one of the poles. Nor does it solve anything to water down or deny the great graces God is giving, or the great need of them that the Church as a whole has. Only by being completely honest, by facing all the facts, by praying much and counseling much, will we be likely to come into God's full purpose in this time of renewal. One thing that is very clear is that the climate of today's Church is very open to pastoral experimentation. It would be a great mistake not to respond to this openness by entering into open and honest dialogue on this question with pastors, bishops, and religious superiors. The situation is more conducive now than at many times in Church history to work out a satisfactory integration of the new with the old. It is important that we openly and honestly communicate with our pastors and bishops and superiors about what's happening by a variety of means open to us: personal conversation, formal report, exchange of literature, etc.

During these years when the foundations and directions of this charismatic renewal are being formed, it is important that we be in maximum communication with one another so that what God desires to bring about may indeed come to fruition. The national conferences, the national newsletter for leaders, the visits we make to one another's communities—all are means by which God can bring us to a unity of mind and heart with his mind and heart, and that can allow him to bring about the true renewal of the Church, and the renewal of the very face of the earth.

For, ultimately, building Christian community, renewing the Church, is something no man does, but something that God himself does. In the end, as in the beginning, it is to the Lord himself that we must turn, and seek his face.

Three Charismatic Communities

Bertil W. Ghezzi

One of the earliest realizations among participants in the charismatic wildfire which burst forth among American Catholics in the winter of 1967 was the need for community life. At Duquesne University and at Notre Dame, men and women who received the baptism in the Holy Spirit immediately began to meet regularly for prayer and sharing. We gathered frequently because we sensed that our growth depended upon it.

We have come to understand that this formation of Spirit-led communities was no accident. Wherever the Lord pours out his Holy Spirit, he draws men together in unity. This is just as true now as it was in apostolic times. As we grow in our understanding of what the charismatic renewal is and where it is going, he continues to deepen our knowledge of the connection between being filled with the Holy Spirit and living as one in the body of Christ.

While participants in the Catholic charismatic renewal often point enthusiastically to scriptural precedents and have learned much from the early Christian assemblies, they do not hold rigidly to them as models. Many of the same elements which appeared in the earliest Christian communities have reappeared in contemporary communities, but in different forms. The biblical models impressed on us the need for such essentials as evangelism, teaching, and pastoral leadership. These areas, however, are developing not according to dictums absolutized in Scripture, but as the Spirit leads us.

The Holy Spirit has given the charismatic communities a variety of structures and experiences. While many share certain likenesses, no two are exactly alike. It is the purpose of this chapter to describe the lives of three different Spirit-led communities in order to show how God has been working with each. None of them is presented as a model Christian community. Each has had some success because of its radical openness to the guidance of the Holy Spirit. This same Spirit who makes us one also gives to each community its unique life and history. Readers, therefore, should not try to duplicate the forms and experience the Spirit has established in the groups included here. They are urged, however, to imitate the attitude of these communities: a consuming desire to please God in everything and to become a full local manifestation of the body of Christ.

Small Prayer Groups

The commonest form which Spirit-led communities have taken is the prayer group. The initial wildfire at both Duquesne University and Notre Dame settled down after a few weeks into small groups which met once or twice a week for praise and sharing. Responding to the same impulse of the Spirit, in the past three years charismatic prayer groups have been formed throughout the North American continent.

Prayer groups normally meet every week. This is a statement of fact, not a formula. Some groups meet monthly or semi-monthly. This is often the case with prayer groups which are sub-groups within larger communities with a weekly prayer meeting. On the other hand, I know of one group whose commitment to the Lord and to each other leads them to meet at 6:30 A.M. daily.

Membership in prayer groups varies according to local circumstances. Many of the original groups in the Catholic charismatic renewal developed within a university environment. They consisted mainly of professors, students, their wives, and a few priests and nuns. That pattern has long since been broken. There are numerous parish groups involving Catholics of every age and background, such as the Grand Haven community described below. The Lansing group, an ecumenical gathering, is like many others across the land which draw together Spirit-filled Christians from different denominations. In Cleveland there is a prayer group for young men and women in high school. There is a priests' prayer group in the Detroit area. The Dominican Sisters at Marywood in Grand Rapids have a regular weekly prayer meeting, as do many men and women religious in houses throughout the country. Whether heterogeneous or homogeneous in composition, the same Lord makes the prayer groups live and work in unity.

Prayer groups vary in size from fewer than ten to more than forty participants (in some instances, many more). Again, this is not a formula. Some groups which desire to preserve a sense of intimate fellowship tend to form new groups once they reach about fifteen members. Others which desire to become fuller Christian assemblies allow their weekly meeting to grow very large and develop smaller fellowship groups as a part of the life of the larger community.

Most of the successful prayer groups have decided at some point to become more than a prayer group. They pledge themselves corporately to become as perfect as possible a local incarnation of the body of Christ. Groups that began as weekly fellowship meetings have become transformed into full Christian communities. In this they are cooperating with what seems to be the Lord's own desire. He has been calling Spirit-filled Christians to share the whole of life together, a life in which the prayer meeting is only one part.

Prayer groups become communities when certain essentials develop. These include the raising up of men and women who perform the services of pastoral care for the community, of sound charismatic teaching and of leading people into the fullness of life in the Spirit and the community.

The Grand Haven Community

To provide a closer look at the life and growth of a prayer group, I have chosen to describe the one I know best, a community of Catholics in Saint Patrick's Parish, Grand Haven, Michigan. Saint Patrick's is a fairly large parish (about 800 families) and Grand Haven is a fairly small industrial-resort town (population 12,000) situated on Lake Michigan, thirty-five miles west of Grand Rapids. I have selected this group for two additional reasons. A description of the Grand Haven community illustrates how a weekly prayer group grows and develops into a full Christian community. It also illustrates how a Spirit-filled community can develop as a bud within a larger parent group and achieve a healthy independent life of its own.

The Grand Haven charismatic community was not the result of wildfire, but the fruit of slow, deliberate growth. The group was born quietly in the summer of 1968 when my wife Mary Lou and I began to pray regularly with our close friends Bud Lothschutz, a Grand Haven architect, and his wife Mary. The Lord had impressed it on my wife and me that he wanted to work in this community slowly and simply. He guided us to wait many months before we shared with Bud and Mary the fullness of life the Lord had given us through the baptism in the Holy Spirit. In the meantime God himself prepared them for their own spiritual renewal through articles, books and conversations and discussions with neighbors of a different denomination. When we were finally led to share our testimony with them that winter, Mary Lou and I were thrilled to find our friends open and desirous of this gift of God. Bud and Mary received the baptism in the Holy Spirit at the Michigan Day of Renewal in Williamston on January 19, 1969.

The two couples continued to pray together, and the Lothschutzs joined us frequently at the Grand Rapids prayer meeting which had been going since November, 1967. We began to take interested friends from Grand Haven to this Tuesday gathering at St. Mary's school gym. Soon a Grand Haven sub-community began to bud within the Grand Rapids community. Among this group were our friends Judy and Jake Vermurlen. When Jake, a linotype operator for the *Grand Haven Tribune*, first heard about the charismatic renewal, he was very skeptical. After he attended a few Grand Rapids prayer meetings in the spring of 1969 the Lord wiped away his doubts by beginning to heal him of diabetes, a healing which continues to strengthen his body. This event consolidated the Grand Haven prayer group. We began in the summer of 1969 to hold Wednesday night prayer meetings in Grand Haven in addition to joining the Grand Rapids group on Tuesdays. Bud, Jake, and I served and taught in the Grand Rapids community, receiving training for the work in the Grand Haven group.

In the fall of 1969 we were led by the Spirit to cut the 35-mile-long umbilical cord which connected us to the Grand Rapids group. We made a commitment to build up the Christian community in Grand Haven, especially in our parish. The group met for the better part of 1969 in the Vermurlen living room. When the room grew crowded, the community moved the prayer meeting to the local Knights of Columbus hall.

A person becomes a committed member of the Grand Haven charismatic community when he decides to live a deeper life in the Holy Spirit and to participate faithfully in the main community activity, the Wednesday night prayer meeting. About 25 people from the local parish have made these decisions. This group varies in age from 23 to 70. There are six couples, a handful of men and women who come without their spouses, a few single women and a loving little Italian widow. All are from the middle classes, but they differ greatly in education and occupation. Five or six friends from small towns 50 miles north of Grand Haven have joined regularly in prayer with the local community.

The Wednesday night prayer meeting is a worshiping assembly that glorifies the Lord in prayer, both vocal and silent, in song, sharing, testimonies and teaching. All the charismatic gifts described by Paul in 1 Corinthians 12 are operative in the meeting. Some of the men take turns acting as leader to call the group to prayer and to keep it centered on the Lord. Occasionally we are blessed with a guitarist to enhance our song, but most often we sing our praises without accompaniment. The meetings have no definite format. The Holy Spirit gives each gathering a unique purpose and message.

A few things, however, have become customary. The meeting usually begins with a short exhortation from the leader and a few lively songs of praise. Then the community raise their voices softly in praise of God. Each uses his own words so that the room is filled with a pleasant worshipful murmur. In the context of this praise, the Lord ministers to the group through spiritual gifts, sharing, Scripture, song, silence, teaching, exhortation, and personal prayer.

At a recent meeting, after the group entered into a

deep spirit of praise through tongues, interpretation and prophecy, the Lord reminded the community how he had freed us from sin and death through the death and resurrection of Jesus. One of the men testified to the new freedom from fear and timidity, a freedom that God has given him. A lady visiting from New York bore witness to Jesus for delivering her from many serious hangups. One member was led to read from the Gospel on the passion and another from Romans 6 on repentance. At several points during the murmur of praise, the group broke into singing in the Spirit. All began to sing, some in English, others in tongues, each his own song of worship, the Spirit blending all in uncanny harmony. One of the women rose to thank the Lord for her successful operation and to share with the community that God had spared her older brother's eye which had been threatened by a staph infection. We had prayed for both during the weeks before. After a period of praise and song, many participants raised up prayer requests. The whole community prayed for each intention with confidence and expectation. The teaching for the evening, which one of the men had prepared beforehand, was a call to repentance. The Lord seemed to have tailored it to fit in with the message of the prophecies, sharing and Scripture. The meeting lasted from 8 until 10 P.M. Afterward most of us stayed around for a half-hour or so of visiting and refreshments.

In addition to the prayer meeting, the Grand Haven community has begun to acquire other features which seem to be essential if a prayer group is to develop into a successful charismatic community. There is a service group of eight members which meets weekly for prayer, study and consideration of the life of the community. This team of four couples has taken the responsibility of fostering the growth of the community, teaching, encouraging and counseling members, leading newcomers into a fuller life in the Spirit, and developing community life and the prayer meeting. They are not a group of experts, but a group of strugglers groping out of the darkness to work for the Lord where he is already working. No mistake they have made has been too big for the Lord to undo—and they have made not a few mistakes.

One of the essentials for a successful community which is still somewhat lacking in Grand Haven is an efficient way of initiating people into the fullness of life in the Spirit and the community. At the moment a few of the members of the service group instruct, prepare and pray for persons seeking to reorient their lives to God and to be filled with the Spirit. The service group is praying about and working out a more responsible method of initiation.

The members of the Grand Haven prayer group are gradually becoming more committed to love and serve each other. As this commitment intensifies, the prayer group will be transformed into a true Christian community. The members are learning how to share each other's spiritual and material burdens. The women of the group frequently provide meals for parish families where the mother is sick or recovering from an operation. On several occasions members have quietly helped other members to pay bills they were unable to meet. Two of the families have become households, inviting young women to become a full part of the life of their homes. The Lord is blessing us with a spirit of generosity and openness which is born amid the praise of the prayer assembly and which has begun to flow throughout the daily lives of all.

The Grand Haven community, while it is drawing closer in love, has no desire to close in on itself. We are committed to share our life in the Spirit with the brothers and sisters we have in our local parish. Most of the members of the charismatic community work hard building the parish community. Two are on the parish council, one also heading up the parish liturgical commission.

One is the choir director and teaches high school religion. Two of the women lead the Ladies' Altar Society. Two of the men are active in the Knights of Columbus. One serves on the school board. Six members have been active in the religious education program; one is a full-time catechist on the staff of the parish religious education center. Not a few of the men are readers, servers or ushers for the Sunday liturgy. It is our concern to be channels for the Lord to minister life, light, and truth to the parish community, so that all the people of Saint Patrick's might become more and more perfectly a local incorporation of the body of Christ.

The Grand Rapids Community

Many groups which began as small living room fellowships have completed the transition to becoming full Christian assemblies. These communities vary in size, composition and intensity of life together. I have decided to describe two of these groups which I know first-hand, the Grand Rapids community and the Ann Arbor community. The first is a heterogeneous community that is developing a fairly intensive life together. The second is a homogeneous group of young people—mostly students —which has a flourishing, close common life.

The Grand Rapids community is built around a Tuesday evening prayer meeting in Saint Mary's school cafeteria which draws participants from miles around the city. Saint Mary's is a parish of moderate size located near downtown Grand Rapids. Many of the community's members belong to this parish, and the community's main leader, Father Charles Antekeier, is assistant pastor there. About 70 percent of the membership in the charismatic community are Roman Catholics. The remaining 30 percent belong to different Christian denominations, principally Christian Reformed, Lutheran, Methodist, and Episcopal. Socially, the group is largely drawn from the middle classes and includes more women than men. Members range in age from 14-year-olds to people five times as old. There are about as many from the over-40 generation as from the other side. The Lord has bound together in his love housewives and career women, high school students and the retired or widowed, bankers and factory workers, foremen and college students, sales executives and carpenters, truck drivers and teachers.

The Grand Rapids charismatic community began in November 1967 in the living room of Msgr. Arthur Bukowski, who was then president of Aquinas College. Sister Amata Fabbro, a Dominican theologian and a member of the original Notre Dame group, introduced him to the charismatic renewal. Msgr. Bukowski invited a team of people from South Bend and Ann Arbor to explain the outpouring of the Holy Spirit to interested Catholics in Grand Rapids and to conduct a prayer meeting for them. About 30 men and women gathered for this purpose in his spacious living room on the Tuesday before Thanksgiving. The team included Father Edward O'Connor and James Byrne from South Bend, Steve Clark and Jim Cavnar from Ann Arbor, Sister Amata and myself. Among the participants in this meeting was Father Charles Antekeier who had received the baptism in the Holy Spirit several weeks earlier while praying and sharing with another Spirit-filled priest.

After about an hour of explanation and testimonies from the team, Jim Cavnar led the gathering in prayer. The Lord poured out his Spirit on that assembly in an extraordinary manner. The first charismatic prayer meeting among Catholics in Grand Rapids was one of the most powerful that I have ever shared in. That evening five or six of the participants were baptized in the Holy Spirit and received the gift of speaking in tongues.

This group continued to meet each Tuesday in Msgr. Bukowski's living room. By February 1968 it had grown so large that the monsignor asked half of the group to meet with Father Antekeier at Saint Mary's parish. For a while the two prayer groups struggled on, meeting faithfully on Tuesday evenings. The Aquinas group folded down when the college recessed for the summer in 1968. A remnant of the Aquinas group joined with the Saint Mary's prayer group. The collegiate group did not start up again in the fall. In the early days of the community, when all of us were such neophytes, we learned through this hard experience that it had been a mistake to divide the community resources.

The first year and a half of life in Saint Mary's charismatic community was not all power and glory. The Lord was clearly moving in the prayer group. He was certainly working in a new way in the lives of the 30 or 40 men and women he had drawn together. But he had not yet perfected the praise of the prayer meeting. Often the gatherings, held at that time on the stage of Saint Mary's gymnasium, were full of petition and sentimentality and very little worship. Sharing was frequently self-centered. The Lord had not yet taught the prayer group that the foundation of life together was the crucifixion of the egocentricity of each member.

The Lord had not yet raised up a group of servants with responsibility for pastoral care in the assembly. But when problems cropped up, not once did he fail to provide answers. On one occasion when the group was having some trouble learning about the gift of prophecy, we prayed for guidance from the Holy Spirit, and shortly thereafter a man from California with a real gift for teaching about prophecy visited us and helped our group.

In that first year the Lord had not yet provided the regular charismatic teaching the group required if it were to become a fuller Christian community. The community did not yet have a responsible way of leading people into prayer for the baptism in the Holy Spirit. In short, the Grand Rapids prayer group in its first year was only a prayer group. It was only beginning to learn what it needed to do in order to become a more perfect manifestation of the body of Christ.

Growing into a Full Christian Community

In mid-course of its second year of life together, the Grand Rapids community began to grow in depth. The Lord began to provide the group with the essentials for an effective Christian community. A service group was organized to take pastoral care of the community life. The community discovered more loving and responsible ways of leading people into the baptism in the Holy Spirit. The Lord provided more regular teaching for the community. He purified the praise of the prayer assembly and developed the spiritual gifts, especially prophecy. The community intensified its life together by the formation of numerous sub-communities of various kinds.

The service group began in the winter of 1968 when Father Antekeier and one of the men began to meet weekly to pray for the community. God gave this young priest the burden of prayer for the whole group and a special spiritual gift for caring for its life. In March a few members began to attend the Leaders' Day, held monthly before the Michigan Day of Renewal, where they began to learn how to serve in the community. In the summer of 1969 the service group had grown to a half dozen men and women who met for an hour before the Tuesday prayer meeting to pray, study, and care for the community's needs. As members of the community began to perform some essential services in the prayer meeting (leading the music, teaching, etc.), they were invited to join the service team. By the winter of 1970, 14 men and women were responsible for the pastoral care of the community. They committed themselves to participate in a weekly two-hour meeting on Monday eve-

nings for prayer, study and work and also to attend the
Michigan Leaders' Day. Throughout the winter the Lord
purified the love of this group of workers. As they deepened, so did the quality of life in the whole charismatic
community.

There are now 25 workers on the service team, and
its structure has developed. One team is charged with
leading newcomers to commit their lives to the Lord
Jesus. Their work centers around an explanation of the
charismatic renewal in a talk which one of them gives
after every prayer meeting. A second team is responsible
for initiating people into a deeper life in the Spirit and
the community. The whole group is charged with leading all members to find their service for the community
and for building up sub-communities. Five of the men
present recommendations to this group and have taken
overall pastoral responsibility for the Grand Rapids community.

As the community's understanding of life in the
Spirit increased, it worked out more loving and careful
ways of leading people to prayer for the baptism in the
Holy Spirit. In the earliest days of the Grand Rapids
group, Father Antekeier or one of the laymen explained
the charismatic renewal to newcomers during the first
half of the Tuesday prayer meeting. The newcomers
joined the assembly for the second part, and when it was
finished we publicly laid hands on those desiring to pray
for the baptism in the Holy Spirit. This continued for
many months before we discovered that this was too
hasty and impersonal an approach. We discovered that
some people for whom we prayed did not have a clear understanding of what they were praying for. Some had not
committed their lives to Jesus. Some were seeking the
latest thing in spiritual experience. We also noticed that
many people we prayed for never came back to the assembly and that some who did return never seemed to
go very deep in the Spirit.

One of the first things we did to remedy this was to stop praying for people publicly. We began to invite those who desired prayer for the baptism in the Holy Spirit to come to a separate room after they had heard the explanation talk and had considered it prayerfully for at least a week. This gave us a chance to offer seekers more care and personal attention.

In the fall of 1969 we developed the process a little more. The Lord had shown us the seriousness of what he is doing in the charismatic renewal. We began to see that the baptism in the Holy Spirit was only one part of a process God was using to lead men into union with him. We learned that he intended the baptism in the Holy Spirit to build men into union with each other in a community which would be a local expression of the body of Christ. The community adopted a way of leading people into the baptism in the Holy Spirit based on this newer understanding.

Following the lead of the Ann Arbor and Detroit communities, we invited newcomers who heard the explanatory talk and who wanted to seek a deeper life in the Spirit to hear a second talk the following week. This "preparation" talk gives us an opportunity to prepare people thoroughly and to get to know them better. After this, individuals are requested to have a personal interview with one of the leaders and to pray, share, ask questions and decide whether he is ready to pray for the baptism in the Holy Spirit. If the person and the leader think that he is ready, we pray for him with the laying on of hands the following Tuesday evening.

At the same time we began to ask of those on whom we laid hands to commit themselves to six teachings on growth in the life of the Spirit. We offer these talks in series at 10:00 P.M. after the prayer meeting. These changes established the grounds for genuine growth in the Grand Rapids community. Men and women began to understand what the Lord is doing and to receive more readily and fully the life he pours out. They began to stick to the community because this process built them into its life. The increased teaching, the personal attention and the readying of men's hearts are creating the foundation for a much sounder common life.

As months have passed the Holy Spirit has provided the community with more and better teaching, a gift which was essential to its growth. Several men and women began to build up the community with regular teachings during the prayer meeting. More community members began to commit themselves to attending the Michigan Day of Renewal where they heard talks and shared in workshops every third Sunday of the month. The Grand Rapids community sponsored several teaching days when the whole group heard gifted visiting speakers. A large number of members attended the growth seminars after the prayer meeting. Some participated in a Christian Life Workshop, involving weekly consideration of different aspects of growth in the spiritual life. Beginning in October 1970, members of the Grand Rapids community were asked to commit themselves to a monthly Community Formation Day when they would receive even more systematic and intensive instruction.

The intensity of life in the Grand Rapids community has begun to manifest itself in a variety of common activities. Community members who belong to Saint Mary's Parish hold a Thursday night eucharist and Scripture study which is having no small impact on the spiritual renewal of parish life. A number of subcommunities and smaller prayer groups have been formed among the members. These include the large prayer meeting of the Dominican Sisters at Marywood, a few smaller home prayer meetings in several parishes, and a number of home Bible studies. Many of the members are participating in group reunions, patterned after the Cursillo's weekly review of prayer, study and witness.

Our brothers and sisters at Our Savior Lutheran Church have four charismatic prayer-study groups and a monthly charismatic assembly. Two Methodist groups and a large Christian Reformed community share in the life of Saint Mary's charismatic community.

Two young men, both workers on the service group, have decided to live a common life of prayer and work. They have rented an apartment which has become a center for the community's activities. These two men have dedicated themselves to serve the community and parish as the Spirit leads them. Although only a recent development, this little household has been a source of new vitality for the whole charismatic community.

The Grand Rapids community has grown in three years from a struggling prayer group of 25 to a full Christian assembly of 300 persons. The growth in spiritual depth, in the purity of praise in the assembly, in the tenderness of love among its members, and in the quality of their common life testifies to the power of the Holy Spirit. He is making God's people out of those who once were no people at all.

The Ann Arbor Community

The most developed community within the Catholic charismatic renewal is the community in Saint Mary's Parish at the University of Michigan. The Lord has matured it with special care and used its structure and life to teach other groups. This does not mean that the Ann Arbor group is without spot or wrinkle, because it is not. With all of its flaws, however, the charismatic community at the University of Michigan has exerted a strong influence on the life of other communities and on the direction of the whole Catholic charismatic movement. From the Ann Arbor experience other groups have learned that a pastoral service group, an effective means of initiation, and sound teaching are essential to common life in the Spirit.

The Ann Arbor community was born in late November 1967 at the same time as the Grand Rapids group, but it developed more rapidly. The first Ann Arbor Thursday evening prayer meetings brought ten students together in the apartment of Jim Cavnar, Steve Clark, Ralph Martin and Gerry Rauch, who had joined the staff of Saint Mary's Parish in October. At the end of the fall term the prayer meeting had grown to 125 participants and was held in the basement of the Newman Center. Three years later the Thursday prayer meeting brings together from 400 to 500 persons. Out of the young men and women who have been drawn to this assembly over the years, the Lord has molded a community who love him and each other with pure hearts, fervently.

I am not going to describe the development of every facet of life in the Ann Arbor community. Some of the important developments in the Grand Rapids community already described, such as the formation of a service group, paralleled developments which were first worked out in the Ann Arbor group. It seems more important to deal with certain features of the Ann Arbor community which make a significant contribution to its vitality.

In the first two years of the community's life, hundreds of people from all over eastern Michigan came to the Thursday prayer meetings. It became clear to the leaders in Ann Arbor that an intensive community could not be built to include members who lived miles from town and came in only once a week. In order to cooperate with what seemed to be the Lord's desire to raise up a people in Ann Arbor, a regular Monday prayer meeting was begun in January 1969 for Christians living around the university who were baptized in the Holy Spirit and who were becoming more strongly knit together. This community has drawn together about 200 students and other young men and women who were already sharing their Christian lives in prayer meetings, liturgies, households, common apostolates and in other ways. Most of the members of this core community are Catholic students, but the group includes a number of Protestant students and an increasing number of young non-students.

The central event for the core community is the Monday prayer meeting. This meeting is not a public gathering but an assembly to which one is invited after he receives the baptism in the Holy Spirit and commits himself to the community. The Monday meeting has no definite structure; it usually begins with an exhortation from the leader for the evening and commonly includes spontaneous prayer, manifestations of the charismatic gifts, readings from Scripture, and song. Frequently one of the leaders gives a prepared talk which lasts about 15 minutes. At the end of the meeting new members are introduced and everyone prays for them as they receive them into the community.

The decision to form an Ann Arbor core community has been very significant. It was a response to a call from the Lord. He showed the whole community that it was his purpose to covenant with them in order to accomplish a part of his plan which he is determined to achieve. He called them to agree together on a common life dedicated to pleasing him. The fruit of the decision has been a deep unity and love within the community and a more thorough reorientation of members' lives toward God. The Monday prayer meeting has also given the Ann Arbor community the opportunity to address itself to problems which could not be discussed appropriately in the large public Thursday meeting.

The first contact new members usually have with the Ann Arbor community is within the open Thursday meeting or with some smaller sub-community. A person becomes a member when he receives the baptism in the Holy Spirit and commits himself to the life of the community. Over the past three years the Lord has given the Ann Arbor community an increasingly more effective and loving way of leading people into a fuller life in the Spirit.

As the community matured, it learned that being baptized in the Holy Spirit meant being initiated into a deep union both with God and with other men. It also began to understand that there was much more to Christian initiation than praying for the baptism in the Holy Spirit. The community discovered how important it is to call men to commit their lives totally to Jesus. It began to lead men to reorient their lives completely to God by repenting of their sins. As understanding grew, members found that the Lord was delivering them of fears of habitual sins and of a multitude of hangups. What God has done has been to renew the whole process of Christian initiation, so that when people become members of the Ann Arbor community they effectively put their lives in the hands of the living God.

The current way which the Ann Arbor community employs to lead people into union with God and each other is a series of six one-hour sessions called "Living the Life in the Spirit Seminars." There is a team coordinated by Ralph Martin which offers these sessions before every Thursday prayer meeting. After a person hears an explanatory talk on the charismatic renewal and expresses some desire to enter the full life of the Spirit, he is invited to attend the seminars. Each week when a new group comes to start the seminars, members of the team and others from the community meet with them and stay with them for six weeks. On a given Thursday six different groups meet, all in various stages of completing the sessions. The first three topics presented are: (1) Union with God and with Each Other; (2) Reorienting One's Life to God; (3) Receiving the Baptism in the

Holy Spirit. After each presentation there is discussion, sharing and prayer. At the fourth meeting, the team prays with laying on of hands for all those in the group who are ready to seek and receive the fullness of the Spirit. The fifth and sixth sessions deal with the essentials of growth in the spiritual life and how to deal with problems, trials, and temptations.

The Ann Arbor community has been using the "Living the Life in the Spirit Seminars" since early 1969. They have found that the seminars are very responsible instruments for serving persons seeking the full life in the Spirit. They have also noticed that the seminars build persons into the community through the friendship which grows naturally within the small groups.

Members who complete the seminars are invited to participate in Steve Clark's 12-week course on the "Foundations of Christian Living." Many members avail themselves of this opportunity to deepen their understanding of practical Christianity. I mention this course to show how thoroughly the Lord seems to be renewing Christian initiation, catechesis and education within the Ann Arbor community.

Sub-Communities and Living Groups

The Monday prayer meeting, although the central event in the community structure, is actually only a small part of the members' life together. Many members who live near each other in dormitories or neighborhoods come together regularly in groups which have come to be called sub-communities. In the spring of 1970 there were nine such sub-communities in the Ann Arbor group. These neighborhood groups meet together for prayer, Scripture study, social activities and common apostolic endeavors. Some of them are working hard at building Christian communities within the dorms. All of the sub-communities have been effective at witnessing to Jesus and drawing people to the Lord and into the larger community.

Some members of the community have committed themselves to live in households or living groups. In the spring of 1970 there were four living groups in the Ann Arbor community, and over the summer several new groups were formed. To outsiders who come in contact with the community, the living groups are one of its most impressive features.

The living groups have discovered that it is one thing to love each other in the prayer meeting and quite another thing to love each other 24 hours a day. The Lord has been purifying households in the same way that he purifies Christian marriages, leading all those living together to crucify their selfishness and to love their brothers and sisters with all their faults.

Each living group defines the purpose of their coming to live together. Some of the groups have as a purpose some common apostolic work. For example, one living group of women is responsible for a guest house to provide hospitality for women visitors to the community. Another group of eight men work as an evangelism team around the campus and town. Other groups define the purpose of their household as a living group devoted to prayer and sharing the Christian life. Members of the living group commit themselves to live according to the purpose of the household and to support each other in the common effort. Most of the living groups have a "head" who coordinates the practical and spiritual life of the house.

The members of these groups are discovering how to help each other to grow in faith and love. They have learned how very simple decisions about little matters make a great deal of difference in the quality of life together. For example, during the summer of 1970 four men lived in a household community which performed the service of caring for visitors. They agreed that in their lives together they would not indulge in any cynicism, sarcasm or negative attitudes. They agreed to love each other so radically that they would help each other by bearing each other's faults, by forgiving and seeking forgiveness, by deciding to be joyful, and by exhorting, instructing and encouraging each other in their common Christian life. The Lord manifested a touching and powerful life among these four. He drew 80 visitors to them between June and September, 1970, none of whom could fail to know the love of Jesus in them.

Many members of the community meet in weekly group reunions, sharing their lives with two or three others. This kind of small group sharing is a third kind of sub-group within the Ann Arbor charismatic community.

The Ann Arbor community engages in a wide variety of activities and apostolic services. The group has a vigorous liturgical life. Many celebrate the eucharist daily with the student parish and many pray in common the Office daily, using *Morning Praise and Evensong*. The whole community gathers each September before the term opens for a conference/retreat to prepare it for the new year. There are regular retreats offered for men and women in the community. One of the most extraordinary features of the community is its frequent parties which by their friendly and open spirit have drawn many into the community life.

One of the community's apostolic projects is providing hospitality within the context of living groups. The several guest houses are more than places where visitors can find shelter. Many persons have come seeking only a place to stay and have received in addition love, guidance and help in coming to the Lord. The sub-communities are committed to serve the men and women in their environments. One of the service teams within the community has dedicated itself to proclaiming the Gospel in Ann Arbor and the training of others in evangelism. Individual members of the community are performing a wide variety of apostolic services within the community, in the student parish and in Ann Arbor as the Spirit leads them.

The community provides important services to the Catholic charismatic renewal. The leaders of the Ann Arbor community sponsor an annual leaders' conference for the movement. In addition they often travel to teach in communities all over the country, and they do a lion's share of the teaching at the annual national conference of the Catholic charismatic renewal. Members of the community edit and publish the national newsletter which serves the charismatic renewal.

The Lord has worked swiftly and surely among these young people. He has formed them with special care that they might stand as one, a bright witness to his power and love.

One significant contribution to the renewal of the Church which the Catholic charismatic movement is making is the renewal of Christian community. The calling together of a particular people, of a local manifestation of the body of Christ, is a fresh new thing God himself is doing. He is repeopling the face of the earth. Throughout the North American continent there are hundreds of sister communities to the three described here—from Regina, Saskatchewan to Hollywood, Florida. They are all unique organisms with a structure enlivened by a powerful breath. In order to make these charismatic communities work, the Lord is renewing areas essential for the maturing of the body of Christ—pastoral care, evangelism, teaching, witness and service. The Lord is determined to manifest his power and love in the flesh of the body of Christ with the same glory which he did in the body of Jesus when he walked the earth. What he requires of us is a desire to work with him in building up that body and faithfulness to the leadings of his Holy Spirit.

November 1970

Charismatic Leadership

James E. Byrne

One thing that can be said about the charismatic renewal with certainty is that *something* is happening—
something genuine and deep is happening among a considerable number of Catholics. It is a work of God. There
are many ways in which God works among men—he
holds all creation in existence through his Spirit, he acts
through nature, through men, through institutions. What
I mean when I use the term "work of God" here, though,
is that in some way the experience which has spread from
Notre Dame and Michigan State as a result of the events
at Duquesne in early 1967 represents a *direct* action by
God working through his Spirit. It is important from my
perspective to grasp this distinction.

I emphasize this because it seems to me that if this
is true, there are certain things we can conclude from it
and certain responses we can suggest. This is not the first
time God has intervened in the affairs of men. As a result of what we know of him from nature and from previous interventions, it is possible to ascertain that God's
actions are not sporadic or arbitrary, but are indicative
of God's personal concern for men. In fact, all his actions
speak of his deep love for men. If this charismatic renewal is directly of God, it is related to what God has
done before, because God does not change, nor do his
purposes change. In fact, God's actions are ordered to a
deliberate plan which he had from the beginning of time

187

and which he revealed through the people of Israel, the prophets, and finally (and completely) in Jesus, in whom, as the Apostle Paul said, "all the fullness of God was pleased to dwell" (Col. 1, 19; 2, 9). This plan, Paul insists, God has revealed to us in Christ: "Such is the richness of the grace which he has showered upon us in all wisdom and insight. He has let us know the mystery of his purpose, the hidden plan he so kindly made in Christ from the beginning to act upon when the times had run their course to the end" (Eph. 1, 7–9).

Indeed, as I look back over these last few years, it seems to me to be clear that what is happening is simply what God has promised would happen. I did not see it clearly at first—I was too overwhelmed by *that* experience. I certainly do not see things clearly now—because whenever we seek to discern God's plans, we do so of necessity from a limited—severely limited—perspective. As the psalmist says: "How lofty, then, to my sight are your designs, O God, how vast their sum! If I would count them, they would outnumber the sands; if I could reach their end, I would be with you still" (Ps. 138, 17–18).

Stated simply, this work of God is part of a plan which has been unfolding for several thousand years. This outpouring of the Holy Spirit is directly related to the promise of God. It is through faith in Jesus Christ that these promises are being fulfilled, and specifically it is through faith in Jesus Christ that *this* outpouring of the Spirit has occurred. For, and here we hesitate, in that same passage from the epistle to the Ephesians, Paul concludes: "Now you too, in him, have heard the message of truth and the good news of your salvation, and have believed it: and you too have been stamped with the seal of the Holy Spirit of the promise, the pledge of our inheritance which brings freedom for those whom God has taken for his own, to make his glory praised" (Eph. 1, 13–14).

In the vision of the early Christians the Spirit was important—so much so that upon Paul's first visit to Ephesus, described in Acts, he can ask: "Did you receive the Spirit when you first believed?" But it is also essential to see that the Spirit was poured out by Christ through belief in Christ—that its outpouring is (as Paul says in Romans 8) the first fruit of the redemption which was begun with the passion, resurrection, and ascension of Jesus. It is in Jesus that this particular outpouring in 1967–71 has its significance, because as Paul says, "all the promises of God find their yes in him" (2 Cor. 1, 20). If we are to see any real significance in what has been happening among us, we must look to the source. It is Jesus Christ who baptizes in the Holy Spirit; it is through faith in Jesus that we receive the release of the Holy Spirit.

It is a tragic (and, I believe, finally) a fatal mistake to ignore the implications of this. This particular outpouring of the Holy Spirit is not isolated either in time or space or in purpose. It is part of the same plan which God has been unfolding through his Spirit among men for 2,000 years, and which aims at bringing all things to completion in Christ.

It is true, I believe, that in our time Jesus Christ is searching out the hearts of men through his Spirit as he has in every generation—because this promise was, as Peter said, to all men in all places, and the promises of God are not in vain. Let us understand this: if we are to be involved in Pentecost, it is not Pentecost which we must preach but Christ Jesus, risen and glorified at the right hand of the Father. What our Lord seems to be doing in our times is renewing his Church, deepening her witness and calling her to a deeper unity. This is the work which is so apparent in Pope John and Vatican Council II as well as in the liturgical, biblical, and other related movements. It seems to me that the charismatic renewal is part of those other renewals and, in many ways, a result of them—an answer to the prayers of so many persons.

If, as we believe, God has spoken to us through this renewal, he expects a response. It is not yet something which everyone can hear, but to those with ears and eyes God's hand is apparent in it. Let us recall that God has spoken many times before, and that again and again men have misunderstood him or have been unfaithful to him. This lack of fidelity is a constant theme in the Old Testament. And the history of the Church is likewise filled with spurious movements, initiated by God but misled, and which finally proved to be false to Christ and which did not serve to build his body.

If we are to view this charismatic renewal as something genuinely from God, we must not confine ourselves to thinking about a prayer gathering or speaking in tongues; our vision must be Christ's vision for the redemption of all men. We do the charismatic renewal a grave injustice if we see it only in terms of one experience or of a few hours of prayer a week. If it means anything, it is vitally related to Christ, his Church, and her renewal, and to fail to relate it to our full Christian lives is, I believe, a failure in charity.

Sharing through Leadership

The ability to help others to share this vision and to make it a daily reality is found among leaders in the emerging charismatic communities. Leadership is clearly a gift of God. It is a ministry in the body of Christ. God has always chosen men to lead his people. Without the gift of leadership functioning properly, the body of Christ will be deficient. Now in speaking of such leadership I am using the term in a restricted sense. In one sense it is clear that every mature Christian, as a functioning member of the body of Christ, is a leader. But I am speaking in terms of those people, men and women, whom the Lord has in one way or another called to assume responsibility for prayer groups.

Initially it might be good for the sake of the average reader, to mention that we believe it would be a serious mistake to confuse leadership within such communities with the office of the priesthood. Vatican Council II made the importance of lay leadership clear. I am by no means anti-clerical, but when priests, by mistaking their function in the Christian community, stifle initiative, it must be pointed out. It is a mistake to confuse the function of leadership with priesthood. This does not mean that there is no place for the priestly ministry in charismatic communities; on the contrary, that ministry is becoming more and more clearly centered upon the full proclamation and celebration of the central action of the Christian community, the eucharist.

Since "charism" and "authority" are contradictory terms in the view of some people, truly "charismatic leadership" was difficult for us to learn. At the Second National Conference at Notre Dame in 1968, I remember asking Jim Cavnar to start one of the meetings with a few songs. Because we were running late, I asked him to play for six or seven minutes. Jim smiled and remarked that there certainly had been a change in our attitude over the last year. I was taken aback by his remark and asked him what he meant. He pointed out that a year previously we would have had lengthy consultations about whether to begin the meeting, how to begin it, what songs to sing, and we would have continued "as the Spirit moved" until someone was "moved" to do or say something else. At the time I was too busy to consider the point, but later, as I puzzled over it, I became amazed at the transformation which had taken place in our understanding of what it meant to be led by the Spirit.

This is even more true now when our understand-

ing of leadership in terms of the work of the Spirit has
evolved considerably. On the whole, this evolution cor-
responds to growth in love and seriousness about the
work of the Spirit. I would like to share with you some
of the things that we believe God has been teaching us
about the Spirit and leadership, its significance, what
Christian Spirit-filled leadership is, and the shapes that
it can take in a charismatic community.

In the first place, the Lord has enabled us to come
to grips with some inadequate notions of leadership
which have hampered our response to the Spirit's work.
The one which recurs most often disqualifies the agency
of human leadership or relegates it to a passive role, as
if to say: "Now that the community is being led by the
Holy Spirit, it doesn't need leadership from me." People with this attitude quote such texts as: "They shall
all be taught by God," which our Lord refers to in John's
gospel (Jn. 6, 45), possibly referring to Jeremiah 31, 34:
"And no longer shall each man teach his neighbor and
each his brother, saying, 'Know the Lord.'" They insist
upon "pleasing God rather than men." In the practical
order, this attitude often refuses to accept any limitation
to what it determines to be God's will.

The results of this attitude are most vivid at prayer
meetings where leaders refuse to set a tone of worship,
prayer, and sharing, or even to exercise control for fear
of quenching the Spirit. Such an idea discounts the value
of preparation, planning, follow-up, and systematic teaching—in fact, the whole function of a deliberate pastoral
ministry. No one would deny that we must be led by
God or that we must please God, not men. But these
truths can be taken in a superficial way that does them
great injustice. All too often, they are used by individuals
to justify conduct which causes scandal or concern to
others. In fact, it is part of our responsibility as Christians to edify other men. Paul made it clear to the Church
at Corinth that if meat offered to idols were an occasion

for scandal, it should be avoided (1 Cor. 10, 9–13). And again, Paul says that he is all things to all men for the sake of the Gospel.

For example, with regard to praying over people for the baptism in the Holy Spirit, I believe it is beside the point to insist that this is primarily God's work. That is obviously the case. But God chooses to work through us to spread it, and often through the laying on of hands. There are certainly many persons whose lives are changed by this prayer. But how many have been prayed with without any change? And again, how many began their walk in the Spirit with great enthusiasm, and after a few weeks or months fell off? I am not judging these individuals. Nor am I saying that nothing valid happened. I am saying that I know of many cases where individuals did not persevere because of the failure of other Christians to support, comfort, and encourage them. In a very real sense, this is a failure of leadership.

Another inadequate notion of leadership sees it personified in one or two strong leaders to whom everyone else looks for direction. This could be termed either "clericalism" or "layism," either from a dominant personality or a charismatic figure. It's a matter of "over" and "under" leadership, and the members fail to see that leadership means more than a one-man operation. Frequently there is a failure to grasp that leadership often grows gradually, and that a person can learn to lead.

Sometimes "leadership" is seen only in terms of the individual or individuals who begin and end the prayer meeting. There is an inability to understand that there are different ways in which leadership is exercised. This is true especially of newer communities whose only function may be a prayer meeting. It is then difficult to visualize other functions of leadership.

Early in our charismatic renewal there was a general reluctance among Catholics to lead. It may be attributed to a false notion of humility, or sinfulness, but more likely it was due to a lack of practice because of "clericalism." For some this is true still. For other groups the problem was seeing the need for leadership and trying to set an abstract leadership plan into operation. All of these attitudes contain genuine insights. Often our attitude toward leadership is colored by a reaction from times when "leadership" meant relying on ourselves and our own devices. In this case, reluctance stems from a genuine desire to follow the promptings of the Holy Spirit. For all too often it results from a realization that in the past our actions for God were nothing but our own ideas and designs. In this respect hesitation on our part is, I believe, the result of an earnest desire to wait upon the Lord, and is a healthy sign. The Lord does lead us through his Spirit. To the extent that these notions enable us to recognize this, then they serve us well; but we must realize that at root, at the core, they are inadequate and mistaken understandings of God's purpose, for they are highly individualistic perspectives. In each of them leadership is viewed in a void. There is a failure to see that at a very basic level we are called not as individuals but as a people. The Spirit's work in us is social; it is incorporating us into the body of Christ. As Vatican Council II declared, "It has pleased God . . . to make men holy not merely as individuals, without any mutual bonds, but by making them into a single people" (*Constitution on the Church,* n. 9).

And further, these notions are based on an oversimplification of God's work in a crude manner which fails to respect the order of things. It does not take into account the ways in which God has led men in history. In his plan the role of men and women as leaders has always been significant. The leaders of the Old Testament were not passive figures. God inspired Moses and David to use all their capabilities and to develop others which they didn't have. In the New Testament we find that leadership has a significant role in the community which our Lord founded. The apostles exercised their leadership in active and deliberate ways, making decisions through discussion, sharing, argument, and compromise, and learning by mistakes and by trial and error.

The Leadership of Paul

Rather than tackling the early Church in general, let us consider just St. Paul's leadership. Paul was led by the Spirit, and his epistles offer the portrait of a powerful and forceful leader. Every phase of the life of the churches he founded merited his attention—he comments upon women's headgear as readily as he does upon the eucharist. And, if we accept the pastoral epistles as Pauline, he doesn't hesitate even to recommend a sip of wine to Timothy for a bad stomach.

Nor does he hesitate to reinforce his leadership. He concludes his lengthy passage on spiritual gifts with the admonition, "If anyone thinks that he is a prophet or spiritual, he should acknowledge that what I am writing to you is a command of the Lord. If anyone does not recognize this, he is not recognized" (1 Cor. 14, 38). Paul's leadership does not quench the Spirit; it is the Spirit who leads him in its exercise. And that leadership was principally pastoral. In his first letter to the Thessalonians, he describes his ministry in two ways, as a nurse and as a father, to illustrate his understanding of the nature of his relationship with these people. Like a father and a nurse, Paul watched over his people, longing and working. He writes to the Colossians: "Now I rejoice in my sufferings for your sake, and in my flesh I complete what is lacking in Christ's afflictions for the sake of his body, the Church" (Col. 1, 24). He tells them that the goal for which he toiled, "striving with all the energy which he mightily inspires within me," was "that we may present every man mature in Christ" (Col. 1, 28–29).

This notion of Spirit-led leadership in terms of building Christian communities is a new thing for Catholics in the 20th century. We are coming to recover the vision of cooperating leadership, and we see that it is a gift of the Spirit and that there are ways of cooperating more effectively and learning to lead in building communities. St. Paul compares it to the work of a mason (1 Cor. 3, 10).

Let us not neglect the obvious fact to which the Scriptures bear witness: that the early Christians were a corporate whole and that they understood the work of God to be one of unity and love, and that this work, inspired by the Holy Spirit, operated through functioning leaders to build up the body of Christ. The kind of Spirit-led leadership we are picturing is essential to the work of the Spirit. We have seen that it is one of the primary ways in which God speaks to men. To men such as Jeremiah, more than once the Lord has had to say, "Do not say 'I am only a youth,' for to all to whom I send you, you shall go, and whatever I command you, you shall speak." In our tradition, the role of leadership has always been valued. It has been recognized, for example, that the Spirit speaks to the Church through the bishops and the pope. But it is necessary also to recognize the role of unofficial, spontaneous, and especially charismatic leadership; this is especially true of the charismatic renewal where the Spirit seems to be forming tight-knit communities. In such situations, functioning leadership is necessary if the community is to survive and grow. It would seem correct to say, "Where there is Christian community, the Spirit seeks to raise up leaders." Where there is inadequate leadership, one of the major vehicles through which the Spirit builds communities is not functioning. The Spirit may work in such situations, but his work is hindered. There are too many prayer groups in which the Spirit's work for deeper unity and love is being restricted to superficial matters, in which there is little growth in sanctity and selflessness. A major portion of this failure rests with those who have failed to assume responsibility.

In this sense, leadership is closely related to the very core of our faith. It is close to the heart of Christian community and the Spirit's work, because leadership is not a game we play or a pose we put on; it operates, if genuine, at the deepest level of our relationships with God and one another. It is the way in which some people are called to show and to work out their love for God and for one another. It is the way in which some people are called to "bear one another's burdens and so fulfill the law of Christ."

Our Lord's ministry was one of leadership. In the course of it, he singled out others who were to continue this function. After Pentecost, it is recorded that the early Church members "devoted themselves to the apostles' teaching and fellowship, to the breaking of bread and the prayers" (Acts 2, 42). It is clear from the first part of Acts that the twelve whom Jesus had chosen functioned as leaders, and that among themselves there were leaders. In scanning this topic, of course, we are skirting many issues. I do not wish to raise the questions of episcopal succession, primacy, etc. The point is that there was clear-cut leadership in the Church to which even the charismatic order was submitted. This is best illustrated by St. Paul's dealings with the church at Corinth. He lays down a number of very striking restrictions pertaining to every aspect of the life of that community, including the charismatic order.

Strong leadership existed in the early Christian community and was not inimical to the Spirit. In fact it was inspired by the Holy Spirit. In Paul's churches order was essential: "For," as Paul wrote, "God is not a God of confusion but of peace." And again, "All things should be done decently and in order" (1 Cor. 14, 33. 40). And it was very clear that in his capacity as a leader Paul himself did not hesitate to set the bounds of that order

—for example holding them to only two or three prophets speaking and two "or at the most three" speaking in tongues (1 Cor. 14, 26). It is a mistake to allow 19th- and 20th-century notions of freedom, individualism, and authority to color our reading of Scripture. It seems clear that leadership, an essential characteristic of the early Church, is a function in the body which needs to be exercised.

The Leadership of Jesus

Christian leadership takes its nature from Jesus himself. There are many types of leadership. Some are so essential that the Church has laid hands on them and ordained them as ministers; others are also essential but of different import. All of them, though, take their significance from Jesus.

All too often function is confused with honor in regard to leadership. What a tragic mistake this is, since we speak of a leadership of service—the one or ones who are servants of all others present. To keep this perspective we would do well to recall what our Lord said about "leaders": "The greatest among you must behave as if he were the youngest, the leader as if he were the one who serves. For who is the greater, the one at table or the one who serves? The one at table, surely? Yet here am I among you as one who serves" (Lk. 22, 26–27).

It was Jesus who made the work of Christian leadership clear by teaching and example. He came as a king. He is, as the book of Revelation says, "King of kings and Lord of lords." Yet his kingship was radically different than kingship as generally understood and practiced. His kingship is grounded in love, in obedience; its hallmark is service. He said: "The Son of Man came not to be served but to serve, and to give his life as a ransom for many" (Mk. 10, 45). He expected his followers, especially the leaders, to follow his example. In John's gospel, he set them an example by washing their feet. Those who followed him were called upon to give themselves completely to him, to become, as Paul describes it, slaves of Christ. And this is done by laboring for others. He says: "Truly I say to you, as you did it to the least of these my brethren, you did it to me" (Mt. 25, 40).

As Christians we share in Jesus' kingship. Vatican Council II, remarking upon the threefold nature of Christ's ministry as priest, prophet and king, talked about his kingship primarily in terms of our relationships within the body of Christ. And I think this is very much to the point. It remains true that his kingdom is among us as he proclaimed it, and its fruit is in peace, justice, and harmony. The Old Testament prophecies have been fulfilled in Jesus, and we are seeing them fulfilled in us as we are incorporated into his body.

Jesus' example has implications for Christian community. In any community there are many forms of service (Rom. 12, 6ff.). At the Notre Dame prayer meeting, for example, there are those who pass out song sheets, those who provide name tags, those who help with coffee, those who clean up, those who assist at the introductory session or in the prayer room, those who lead the prayer meeting, and those who teach at the prayer meeting, to name but a few. In this sense Jesus' example has meaning for every mature Christian. And there are some people in every community who assume a general responsibility, who are led to spend time and energy to satisfy overall needs which they see. They are the ones who serve the community as a whole. There are those who plan the functions of the community and organize them. There are also those who are responsible pastorally for sub-groupings in the community. In our community in South Bend we have several sub-groups—a student group, a group with an inner city apostolate, etc. On another level there are people who by their life and example are accepted as teachers. Finally, there are those, usually one or two, who are responsible for the life of the whole community and all of its aspects. Often in smaller or younger communities, these levels are combined in one or several persons. But they rapidly begin to emerge as separate, distinct and necessary functions. A pastoral ministry is vital on each of these levels, although its form and significance vary. The general concerns of pastoral leadership should be mentioned at this point.

Areas of Leadership

One such area of concern involves those who are emotionally or psychologically disturbed. The charismatic renewal tends at times to attract a number of individuals who may be unbalanced. This is an indication of the Lord's presence. Jesus loves the poor and the sick. But the presence of these people requires strong and effective leadership. Although most of us have problems, some people have difficulties whose nature renders them unable to judge and function normally. This isn't always obvious at first sight. Frequently such an individual will seem to have a deep spirituality and to be especially open to the Spirit. Such an individual may be attracted toward an active role in the community, even of leadership. Gradually, though, irregularities will surface. Although it is rarely clear, there will be grounds for suspicion. Many actions may seem to be authentic and an individual may say good things at a prayer meeting, but often the remarks will be out of context or distorted, and the actions will fail to bear fruit. At this point leadership is essential. Those who have noticed irregularities must have the courage and the charity to ask questions which need to be asked. Sometimes this can be done singly, sometimes in groups; at times people have been asked not to speak or even to attend meetings. Where openness and good will exist, healing prayer or deliverance can have amazing results, but where the person is unable to recognize the existence of the problem, the door through which Jesus would place his healing hand is locked. As communities we must grow to the point where we can give others the love and attention they need. Often such people require close attention. Leadership must be alert to all of this.

Another area of concern is in the exercise of the spiritual gifts. Some communities do not experience freedom in the charisms, and in many others only one or two individuals are charismatic. Rather than simply attributing this to God's will, often there is a need for leaders to teach people about the gifts and to offer instruction about exercising them. Often false notions, a sense of unworthiness, and doubts need to be dealt with. People need to be encouraged to grow in the exercise of the gifts. Where the gifts are abused, as with false prophecy, there is a need for leadership to help the individual recognize this and perhaps purify the gift. Leaders must be sensitive to whether the charisms lead to a growth in love. Often they are only "prayer meeting gifts" because members of the community cannot envision how they relate to other situations. It is the role of the leader to share such vision with them.

Prayer meetings themselves are areas in which leadership is crucial. When prayer meetings begin to drag and there seem to be essential elements lacking, the leader must act. There may be periods of strained silence (quite different from meditative, peaceful silence). Or perhaps all of the elements are present but in such a way that no one is built up. There is a need for leaders to begin to pray and study and share ideas about this. Sometimes there is a need for witness, sometimes a need to preach the Gospel. The leader is the one who begins to face these needs through his own example, perhaps sharing his testimony, and then through urging others. The one

who begins to notice an area of need may be the one the
Lord wants to use to make the community aware of the
need. For example, if there is too much singing and if
after several weeks you note that someone begins songs
which interfere with what the Lord is doing, he should
be taken aside and told, or perhaps there is a need for a
general teaching about the role of singing in worship.

Do you feel that your prayer group has reached a
plateau where the prayer seems hollow, where some people are slipping away and others have doubts? Perhaps
there is a need for teaching about the means to growth
in the Christian life. Growth is yet another area of pastoral concern. Possibly few people have heard about the
need for daily prayer and Scripture study and witnessing;
perhaps few have committed themselves to these activities.
How many people who come to prayer meetings are
growing in charity? Are they growing in sanctity? What
about a regular prayer life? Have people been encouraged in this? What about their neighbors, wives, hus-
bands, families, society—is there a marked growth in
love here? There is a real danger in this area of people
confusing the attendance at prayer meetings with the
work of God. The phenomenon of prayer meeting "hop-
ping" is one which can easily lead to irresponsibility to
God and to men. It often leads to seeking spiritual experiences rather than seeking to pour ourselves out in
the service of God and men.

The work the Holy Spirit is doing is much deeper
than a few nights (or every night) at a prayer meeting.
The work of leadership has very definite, concrete, pastoral implications. It may or may not involve organization; it always involves love and concern and always is
the work of the Spirit. It is a function of the body—in a
sense, the most demanding one.

Leading others to seek a fuller life in the Spirit
should be regarded as a mission with which God has entrusted the charismatic communities. It should be ap-

proached with "fear and trembling" lest anyone be led astray. The need for pastoral ministry within a prayer group is usually awakened by a need to teach newcomers at prayer meetings about the charismatic renewal. It is a critical function of leadership to find an organized, responsible approach to introducing others to the baptism in the Spirit and providing for continued formation. A systematic approach to this task within a community can function to bring people together and give them the opportunity to serve and be served. Such an approach will make sound teaching possible by encouraging those with this ministry to study, share and pray. It will embolden those whose gifts are concerned with ministering the baptism in the Holy Spirit by providing them with experience and mutual support. It will provide newcomers with an opportunity to understand the charismatic renewal and to seek the Spirit themselves. While an organized approach will in no way ensure these results automatically, it can be an opportunity for serious and prayerful Christians to provide the Spirit with a vehicle through which to work more effectively.

The Ministry of Initiation

Because this pastoral ministry is usually the first to arise within a community, it would be wise to define in detail how such a plan would concretely function before continuing with more general remarks on pastoral care.

Initially, we view such a program, based upon the two natural steps of instruction and prayer, as distinct from the prayer meeting. Although in a community's initial stages these functions are often combined with the prayer meeting, the group cannot continually offer such an opportunity in any depth. What a prayer meeting can indicate is that something has happened. A distinct introductory session can indicate more precisely what has happened and why it has happened in order to show how it can happen again. Such sessions can be simultaneous with the prayer meeting, or they can precede it or follow it.

A second stage in this development is to designate responsible members of the community to conduct the introductory sessions. In the first stages of the pentecostal experience such a program is spontaneous and frequently the work of any member of the community who happens to attend. As the significance of the introduction comes to be recognized, and as those who are accustomed to work in the sessions become more experienced, certain members of the community are designated to conduct this apostolic effort. Another step is reached when these individuals, as a result of common experience and growth in charity, are able to specify certain ministries and to work together as a team. Such cooperation enables the members to concentrate in their particular ministries and permits the team to focus its attention more fully on the needs of those attending the session.

The third stage in the development involves a distinction between instruction about the baptism in the Holy Spirit and the prayer to receive it. Such a distinction generally can be observed even when the two functions are performed at one session. A corollary of such a distinction and an indication of the seriousness with which it is viewed is seen in the rule that *instruction must precede prayer*. Although no community presumes to claim a monopoly on the Holy Spirit, there is a recognition of common responsibility. The Holy Spirit is always free to work spontaneously, and he often does. But when a community joins with an individual in prayer for the baptism in the Holy Spirit it has a responsibility not to take such prayer lightly or to allow that person to do so if possible. To do so would be close to blasphemy.

Several styles of instruction can be distinguished. As

the community grows, each is used more skillfully to provide a balanced presentation.

1. Testimony is an important part of an instruction session. It provides a concrete instance of the work of the Holy Spirit through the charismatic dimension. Often it enables those present to understand the scope of the Spirit's work and to identify it with their situation.

2. Exhortation is another style of instruction. Its charismatic quality may be more visible than that of explanation or testimony. Its purpose is to stir up the faith and charity of those present and to encourage them to seek God more fervently.

3. Explanation complements testimony and undertakes the essential task of defining the baptism in the Holy Spirit and its relation to the Church, her sacraments and her spirituality. The character of the explanation is determined by the training and requirements of a community.

Some other areas to be treated in any introductory session might include a brief background or history of the charismatic renewal, both in the whole Church and in the local community. The charisms also should be treated in light of Scripture, the teaching of the Church and experience. Their service function should be outlined, as should the fact that they are not necessarily an indication of personal sanctity. The gift of tongues usually requires special treatment because it is the gift which attracts most attention and is most open to misunderstanding. Its function as a gift of prayer, of praise as well as petition for the Christian assembly and for the upbuilding of the individual, should be described.

The fruits of the Spirit should be mentioned. The fundamental significance of the fruits of the Spirit's presence and actions deserves emphasis. Examples from the lives of members of the community will illustrate this point. Given adequate time and a competent teacher, the relationship between the charismatic experience and the tradition of the Church could be treated. This should be done specifically with regard to the Church, her hierarchy, her sacraments, her teachings, her saints, and her spirituality. In this regard, it is helpful to recall the privileged place which the Church has accorded the Holy Spirit in her teaching and her spirituality. These words of Pope Paul VI give an apt summation of the Church's position: "The Church's first need is always to live Pentecost."

Specifically "pentecostal" practices such as the laying on of hands, or of binding or testing the spirits, might also need clarification.

The Need for Continuing Formation

The apostolate of leading others into the baptism in the Holy Spirit is itself a distinct phase of the broader apostolate. It is a genuine expression of love. That it represents the major, primary apostolic thrust of most prayer communities as such is fitting. In sharing the experience of the baptism in the Holy Spirit they are doing a great service for the Church. This experience touches the very heart of the renewal which the Church has undertaken. But it should be clear that a person who receives the baptism in the Holy Spirit will need additional formation, whether basic or advanced. Such formation is essential for growth. Those who have come to Christ for the first time will need a solid foundation in prayer, doctrine, and the apostolate. Those who have been living the Christian life will need to integrate the charismatic dimension into their spirituality and to deepen their life in Christ. Such formation does not just happen. And in most cases the prayer meetings of themselves do not provide sufficient opportunity for this. That is not their primary aim, although teaching is an aspect of the meetings. It is necessary, therefore, for those responsible for the others to realize that, in addition to introductory work, opportunities must be provided for the Spirit's work of formation.

The first step in formation involves continued contact with those who pray to receive the baptism in the Holy Spirit. In smaller groups such contact may be natural, but in larger groups it is necessary to delegate the responsibility to keep in touch with individuals. One of the most reasonable suggestions I have heard in this area is to ensure this through a "sponsor" system. Each person in the prayer room would then have a sponsor who would assist in prayers, talk with the person after the meetings and visit and contact him during the week. By sharing experiences, both sponsor and friend will grow together. This system provides relatively new members of a community with an ideal opportunity to learn to assist others while at the same time growing in faith.

As the need for more formation becomes clearer and as communities grow, a need may be seen for a series of seminars. Basic Christian instruction should include general facets of the Christian life such as Christ, faith, growth, community, apostolate, and charisms. Advanced seminars should treat the integration of the charismatic experience into the whole of Christian life.

Until the community undertakes such a project, opportunity for the individual's formation should be encouraged through spiritual direction where possible, through responsible Christian friends, literature, and specific tools such as the Cursillo or the Antioch Weekend.

In all of these areas, there is a need for leaders to seek ways of service. It is a mistake to think that the Spirit will give you a blueprint. This is not the kind of leadership that the Spirit inspires. Usually needs are sensed obscurely, and it is only after thought, discussion, and trial and error that solutions can be effected. The kind of leadership that God expects us to provide is often discovered in our half-blind responses to needs. And the service primarily required is a general concern for the growth of individuals and the community. It is the role of pastoral leadership to discern that which edifies and to encourage it, and to discern that which divides and discourage it. This kind of leadership does not arise automatically. It usually begins with a few concerned individuals. People begin to compare notes, to feel moved to pray and share together outside of the context of the prayer meeting. Such emerging core communities within the community usually need a regular opportunity for prayer, discussion and teaching.

Notions of core groups, ministries, meetings and such should not obscure the importance of Christ-centered friendship between leaders which they are designed to deepen. Though forms can be copied, the lessons of trust, love and loyalty must be learned by all.

Qualities of Leadership

Leaders are often the most unlikely people. Though natural talent is a strong foundation stone, the principal characteristic seems to be willingness, a radical openness to God and a desire to take him seriously, to be responsible to him. Such leaders emerge from groups; their failure to do so usually, though not always, means the failure of the group. It always means ineffectiveness. The second characteristic is faithfulness. Let me call your attention to these words of our Lord: "He who is faithful in a very little is faithful also in much, and he who is dishonest in a very little is dishonest also in much" (Lk. 16, 10).

A leader needs many talents. It is not enough to know this technique or that one. There are few keys to Christian leadership. It is necessary to learn to apply our whole mind and heart to the Lord.

A leader needs to accept the cross. The battle we

wage is against powers and principalities, and the leader is at the forefront of the battle. We must heed our Lord's words: "If any man would come after me, let him deny himself and take up his cross and follow me. For whoever would save his life will lose it, and whoever loses his life for my sake will find it" (Mt. 17, 24–25). And again: "A servant is not greater than his master. If they persecuted me, they will persecute you" (Jn. 15, 20).

A leader needs to be concerned with his own spiritual growth as well. St. Paul wrote: "I pummel my body and subdue it, lest after preaching to others I myself should be disqualified" (1 Cor. 9, 27). As leaders we need to be especially aware of the kind of spiritual hypocrisy which lets us lead others while we are not growing in holiness. If we as leaders do not even pray regularly, how can we lead others to God? "The servant who knows what his master wants, but has not even started to carry out those wishes, will receive very many strokes of the lash. . . . When a man has had a great deal given him, a great deal will be demanded of him; when a man has had a great deal given him on trust, even more will be expected of him" (Lk. 12, 47–48).

What we need are men and women with the vision of the kind of body that the Spirit is forming, whose eyes are fixed on Christ Jesus and whose hearts long for the fullness of Christ. They must be generous in the giving of themselves and willing to make commitments. Their concern must be primarily for God's people. The work of pastoral leadership has concrete, day-to-day, flesh-and-blood implications. It is not glamorous, but I believe it is an intentional and integral part of God's economy of salvation. Though he certainly did not need men to lead his people, he chose to work through them. Such a fact might well fill us with awe and cause each of us to echo David's words: "Who am I, O Lord God, and what is my house, that thou hast brought me thus far?" Yet it has been true from the time of Moses until the present that God has worked through leaders to lead his people, be they prophets, priests, apostles, saints, bishops, or laymen.

Without the gift and function of leadership, the body of Christ will be the poorer. Its exercise requires many of the gifts of the Spirit. It involves a certain God-centered restlessness, a constant looking at things and asking how they could be better. It is a ministry of looking for the best in every situation. It is not a matter of setting up instruction rooms or organizing conferences. It is not a matter of *doing* things at all. It is a matter of loving. It must be done in love, out of love for God and man. Any other motive will fall short. The Spirit's call to leadership is none other than a call to a deeper love and responsibility—a call to plunge more deeply into the life and love of the Spirit.

Toward the end of St. John's gospel he records an incident between the Lord and Peter. The question the Lord asks of Peter challenges us as well: "Do you love me?" As we say "Yes, Lord, you know that I love you," he replies: "Feed my sheep."

The Charismatic Movement: 1967–1970

James Connelly, C.S.C.

On the weekend of April 7–9, 1967 about a hundred students from the University of Notre Dame and Michigan State University, along with several priests and some laymen who at the time were Cursillo leaders in Lansing, Michigan, South Bend, Indiana, and Cleveland, Ohio, gathered on the Notre Dame campus for what has been dubbed in retrospect the First Annual National Catholic Pentecostal Conference. The weekend itself was spent in prayer, with the group alternating between prayer meetings which lasted for several hours at a time and the celebration of the eucharist.

What brought these people together was the belief that in the weeks preceding this weekend they had come into an experience of the power and love of God which they had learned from friends in the pentecostal churches to refer to as the "baptism in the Holy Spirit." [1] They testified to something having happened to them which was radically changing their lives, but they were not quite sure what it was. Many acknowledged that this experience had brought a deep and abiding joy; several confessed to its having been the occasion for a real conversion on their part. At the same time there was a note of anxiety. Some were afraid of what friends and family, not to mention the general public, would say. Many were concerned lest their respective bishops order them to cease and desist.

The story of how these people first came to hear about and seek the baptism with the Holy Spirit has been told elsewhere.[2] Prior to this weekend, individual Roman Catholics had come into this experience, and there was at least one such community of Catholics centered around Duquesne University in Pittsburgh. The significance of this weekend for the story which follows, and what recommends it as the starting point for an account of the Catholic pentecostal movement, is the impetus which it gave to a wide variety of factors. It was probably the first time that Catholic pentecostals from different localities gathered together to share their experience with and encourage one another. It was attended by many of those who in the next few years would be the key "missionaries" of the charismatic renewal among their fellow Catholics.[3] The experience of this weekend illustrated the importance of communities or prayer groups for Catholics who were becoming involved in the charismatic renewal; as these were formed by and through the participants in this weekend, they continued to keep in communication with one another, visiting frequently and gathering together, regionally and nationally, at regular intervals.

The weekend further qualifies as a beginning point for the story of the movement because it attracted the attention of the press. *The Notre Dame Scholastic* and *The Observer,* student publications, carried sensational stories of the weekend which attracted large crowds to the Notre Dame prayer meetings in the weeks immediately following. These stories provoked comment in the local diocesan press, and *The National Catholic Reporter* did a story on the happenings at Notre Dame which gave them a national advertisement. Articles also appeared in *Ave Maria,* a national Catholic weekly.[4]

One immediate result of all this publicity was to

arouse the interest of many who were coming to Notre Dame for the summer session in 1967. On June 30 five Catholics from Notre Dame, Bertil Ghezzi, Kevin and Dorothy Ranaghan, Sister Amata Fabbro, O.P., and Father Edward O'Connor, C.S.C., held an open meeting in the auditorium of the Notre Dame Law School to introduce the charismatic renewal to those summer school students who were interested. Several days later prayer meetings began to be held twice weekly on the Notre Dame campus and these continued throughout the summer session. Many students and visitors from all parts of the country attended the meetings and went back home to begin prayer groups themselves or to spread the word of what was happening at Notre Dame.[5]

The Campus Phase

Throughout the rest of 1967 people on college campuses proved to be the most receptive audience for the message of what had happened at Duquesne, Notre Dame, and Michigan State. Press coverage of Catholic pentecostals also highlighted the activities on college and university campuses, and the impression still persists in many quarters that the Catholic pentecostal movement is something for college students. Though the movement quickly ceased to be confined to campuses, students have, as a group, continued to account for a large part of the membership in the movement and to be instrumental in presenting it to others. With this in mind an account of the "campus phase" of the movement's expansion seems to be in order.

Two of the Notre Dame students who were present at the April weekend, James Cavnar and Gerald Rauch, had been active in putting on Antioch Weekends, closed weekend retreats for college students. In the spring of 1967 Cavnar and Rauch went to Ames, Iowa, to put on

an Antioch Weekend there for Catholic students at Iowa
State University. While in Ames they told a number of
people about what had been happening at Notre Dame.
Several students then asked to be prayed over that they
might receive the baptism in the Holy Spirit, and by the
end of their visit a Catholic pentecostal community had
been set in motion among the Iowa State students.
Michael Fitzgerald and Peter Collins, who had worked
on the Antioch Weekends while undergraduates at Notre
Dame, were working as extension volunteers at the Catholic student parish at the University of Colorado in Boulder, Colorado, in the spring of 1967. From Cavnar and
Rauch they heard about the events at Notre Dame; Ralph
Martin and Stephen Clark, assistants to the Catholic
chaplain at Michigan State University, informed them of
similar happenings on the East Lansing campus. Their
interest aroused, they began to inquire further, and by
the end of the summer they too had experienced a release of the Spirit, had spoken in tongues and were introducing others to the experience. Subsequently another
community arose in Boulder.[6]

One of those whom Fitzgerald and Collins introduced to the baptism of the Spirit was Father Edward
Keefe from St. Ambrose College in Davenport, Iowa. Returning to Iowa in September 1967, Father Keefe made a
retreat at the Trappist Abbey of New Melleray near
Dubuque, Iowa, where he told the monks what he had
heard in Colorado and held several prayer meetings with
them while he was at the monastery. In the summer of
1968 Rev. Ray Bringham of Inter-Church Team Ministry
and Father Francis MacNutt, O.P., visited New Melleray
and prayed with the monks, many of whom were baptized with the Spirit.[7] Father Keefe was later assigned
to the staff of the Catholic chaplaincy at the University
of Iowa in Iowa City, where he was joined in the fall of
1968 by Fitzgerald and John Clarke. These three be-

came the nucleus of a Catholic pentecostal community in Iowa City.

Father Charles Harris, C.S.C., of the University of Portland in Portland, Oregon, was informed of what had been happening at Notre Dame and elsewhere when he came to the Notre Dame campus in the summer of 1967 to work on a revision of the manual for the Antioch Weekend. When he returned to Portland in the fall, he and Edward Kaiel, a student who had visited Clark and Martin in Lansing, told others about what was happening, and prayer meetings were begun which became charismatic during the following months.[8]

At the end of the summer many of the people who had attended the April weekend came together again on the Notre Dame campus for a conference on the campus apostolate and the Antioch Weekend. Many people from the Duquesne community were present, as were a number of people from around the country who had heard of the conference and were in some way involved with the charismatic renewal. Rev. Edward Gregory and Rev. Robert Beckett, representing Inter-Church Team Ministry, an interdenominational group of ministers who worked at making the charismatic renewal better known and accepted in the mainline Protestant churches, attended and addressed the conference, as did Rev. Lloyd Weber, a United Church of Christ pastor and leader of a pentecostal community in a Chicago suburb. This conference provided those present with the opportunity to share their experiences of the summer and thereby to take stock of what was happening. The theme of the conference was how to present the Gospel to others— "bearing witness"; coming at this time, it had much to do with making this a major concern of the communities which were just beginning to take shape and whose leaders were in attendance.[9]

Two people who had played prominent parts in the

April conference at Notre Dame were Ralph Martin and Stephen Clark, both Notre Dame alumni. They had been responsible for bringing word of what had happened at Duquesne to the Michigan State campus, where they were assisting the Catholic chaplain. Upon returning from the April weekend at Notre Dame they continued to serve as leaders of the Catholic pentecostal community which was forming in Lansing and East Lansing. Many of the members of this community were students. When they dispersed for the summer vacation, word of what had happened at Notre Dame and Michigan State was carried to many parts of the state of Michigan. In the summer of 1967 Martin and Clark were joined by Cavnar and Rauch, who had graduated from Notre Dame in June. The four originally intended to work as a team assisting the Catholic chaplain on the Michigan State campus, but they were advised late in the spring that they would not be hired in that position. At the end of the summer they accepted an invitation from the Catholic chaplain at the University of Michigan in Ann Arbor to work with him on that campus, and they moved there in September. As they began to tell people of what had happened in Pittsburgh, East Lansing, and South Bend, a community formed around them in Ann Arbor, meeting at first for prayer in their apartment, and moving to the Catholic student center when the numbers became such that the apartment could no longer hold them.

Since the fall of 1967 the Ann Arbor community has become something of a model and a place of pilgrimage for many Catholic pentecostals. As of this writing, its Thursday night prayer meetings regularly attract several hundred people, some of whom drive many miles to be present. It has played host to many distinguished visitors, including several bishops and at least one cardinal. Its leaders are in demand as speakers all over the country. Like other communities with large student contingents, its members have served as missionaries of the charismatic renewal in many parts of this country and abroad.

Other Beginnings

Meanwhile, in August 1967, Father Francis Mac-Nutt, a Dominican priest from St. Louis who at the time was the executive secretary of the Christian Preaching Conference, attended a seminar on the healing ministry sponsored by the Camps Farthest Out in Maryville, Tennessee. The seminar was conducted by Mrs. Agnes Sanford, the widow of an Episcopal priest, Tommy Tyson, a Methodist minister who had worked with Oral Roberts, and Derek Prince of the Holy Spirit Teaching Mission in Fort Lauderdale, Florida. Father MacNutt had read some articles on the events of the previous spring at Notre Dame, but he had had no contact with the Duquesne-Notre Dame-Michigan State movement. In the course of the seminar he received the baptism in the Spirit and spoke in tongues. Returning to St. Louis, he participated in an ecumenical prayer group during the fall of 1967 and the winter of 1968. He also accepted many invitations to address meetings of the Full Gospel Business Men's Fellowship International (F.G.B.M.F.I.), an interdenominational layman's organization, and in this way made many contacts with Protestants and individual Catholics who had associated themselves with the Full Gospel Business Men.

Traveling extensively as a retreat master, Father Mac-Nutt has been responsible for introducing many Catholics to the charismatic renewal, especially in the western and southwestern states, as well as in Peru and Guatemala where, in the spring of 1970, he joined with three Methodist ministers to give charismatic retreats for missionaries. Largely as a result of his efforts, a Catholic pentecostal community formed in St. Louis in the fall of 1968.[10]

On October 7, 1967 a woman living in the vicinity of St. Benedict's Abbey, a Benedictine monastery in Benet Lake, Wisconsin, gave one of the monks a tape of a talk given by Father O'Connor of Notre Dame to a meeting of the Full Gospel Business Men. The tape aroused the interest of several of the monks, and they agreed to attend an evening of Bible study in the woman's home. In short order four of the monks received the baptism in the Spirit and spoke in tongues. Shortly thereafter the abbot and several of the monks attended a charismatic seminar at the Church of the Good Shepherd in Elk Grove Village, Illinois, a Chicago suburb, where Kevin Ranaghan of Notre Dame was one of the speakers. Ranaghan told them what had been happening at Notre Dame and elsewhere, and the group from Benet Lake returned to the monastery favorably impressed. Ranaghan and O'Connor visited the abbey in early December at the abbot's invitation and spoke at length to the monks on the experience of other communities and individuals over the preceding months. They discussed the baptism in the Spirit and charismatic gifts with them in an effort to allay the opposition of some of the members of the monastic community.[11]

The monks who had received the baptism in the Spirit continued to attend prayer meetings in the homes of various denominational pentecostals in the vicinity of the monastery and they also began to spread the word of what they had experienced among many Catholics in the neighborhood. In March, 1968, at the request of one of the Catholic laywomen whom the monks had told about the baptism in the Spirit, open weekly prayer meetings were begun at the monastery, and by the summer of 1968 crowds of more than 100 persons, some coming from as far away as Chicago and Milwaukee, were attending these meetings. One of the Benedictines, Father David

Geraets, began teaching at Dominican College in Racine, Wisconsin, in the fall of 1968 and told a number of the faculty and students what had happened at the monastery. Several of them asked him to pray with them that they might receive the baptism in the Spirit; these formed the nucleus of a Catholic pentecostal community in Racine.[12] In the fall of 1969 five monks from the monastery at Benet Lake went to Pecos, New Mexico, to reorganize the 14-year-old priory of Our Lady of Guadalupe as an experimental pentecostal community.

In the summer of 1966, Stephen Clark of Ann Arbor and Theodore Sohn of New York City had visited John Sherrill, the author of *They Speak with Other Tongues,* a popular account of the charismatic movement. Sherrill spoke to them about the baptism in the Spirit but suggested that they go off and pray for it on their own. In the summer of 1967 Sohn visited Clark in Lansing, attended several prayer meetings while there and received the gift of tongues. When he returned to New York he shared his experience with others, and two prayer groups, one on Long Island and one in Brooklyn, formed. Clark was employed by the national office of the Cursillo movement and in this capacity attended a Cursillo de Cursillos in Garrison, New York, for the northeastern Cursillo centers in early December, 1967. Several of the Brooklyn Cursillo leaders had adopted the practice of meeting one evening a week to pray together. Two of these invited Clark to attend their evening meeting after the Garrison weekend. On that evening he spoke to them about the charismatic gifts as listed by St. Paul in the twelfth chapter of 1 Corinthians and related the things which had been happening at Notre Dame and Ann Arbor. Three of the people present asked Clark to pray with them for the baptism in the Spirit and they received it. This was a turning point for the Catholic pentecostal community in Brooklyn. In the summer of 1968 Father James Powers, S.J., one of those with whom Clark had prayed, formed another community at Fordham University in the Bronx which served to introduce many of those attending the summer session at Fordham to the charismatic renewal. Among the students at Fordham that summer were several nuns from Baltimore who were instrumental in beginning a Catholic pentecostal community in that city upon their return in the fall.[13]

On October 15, 1967 two dozen Catholics who had been baptized in the Spirit came together from various points in Michigan for a day of prayer, study and fellowship. This meeting, which proved to be the first monthly Day of Renewal for Catholic pentecostals in Michigan, assembled that day in the living room of Mr. and Mrs. James Rauner of Williamston, a small town east of Lansing. After three months the Rauner's house was no longer adequate, and in January 1968 the Day of Renewal was moved to the parish hall of Saint Mary's Church in Williamston where it was held for more than a year; later it was transferred to one of the Catholic high schools in Lansing. The informal schedule of that first Day of Renewal has become a customary format: Bible vigil, sharing session, a talk, workshops, supper and a prayer meeting to end the day. As of April 1970, crowds of 700 or 800 were not uncommon for the Mchigan Day of Renewal.[14]

To the Day of Renewal, held on the third Sunday of the month, was eventually added a Leaders' Workshop held on the preceding Saturday at which those who had taken on responsibility for the various communities gathered to address themselves to some pastoral concern. In March 1969 the publication of a pastoral newsletter summarizing the talks and discussions of these Saturday workshops was begun; by March 1970 this publication had attained a circulation of nearly 800 copies. With the issue of June 1970, its scope was broadened to make it a newsletter serving the charismatic renewal among Catholics in the United States and Canada.[15]

A Day of Renewal, following more or less the format of the one in Michigan, has become a useful and widely imitated institution among Catholic pentecostals. A monthly Day of Renewal was begun in Cleveland in the spring of 1969, in the New York City area in July 1969, in Albuquerque, New Mexico, in Benet Lake, Wisconsin, and in New Orleans in the fall of 1969. Other areas have held such days on an irregular basis.

1968: The Circle Widens

By the beginning of 1968 there were at least fourteen Catholic pentecostal communities in the country. There was much visiting back and forth between the communities in Pittsburgh, Ohio, Indiana, and Michigan, and a loose network of communication based on personal friendships had been established, as had the practice of holding Days of Renewal. Throughout the fall of 1967 and the winter of 1968 several of the Catholics involved in the charismatic renewal began to appear as speakers at F.G.B.M.F.I. dinners and conventions and to work with the Inter-Church Team Ministry. In this way news of what was happening among Catholics spread in these circles.

The Second National Catholic Pentecostal Conference, billed at the time as a "Holy Spirit Weekend," assembled on the Notre Dame campus on the weekend of March 29–31, 1968. It brought together again, for the first time since the previous September, most of those who had been present for the weekend in April, 1967. In addition, people from around the country were present, including a large contingent from Florida led by Dr. Susan B. Anthony. Mr. and Mrs. John Leary came from New Mexico, Father Walter Hanss from Rochester, Father William Manseau from Boston and Father Killian McDonnell, O.S.B., from Collegeville, Minnesota.[16] Many of these same people gathered at the Bergamo Center in Dayton, Ohio, for a seminar on the charismatic renewal from May 30 to June 2, 1968. Every bishop and major religious superior in the United States was invited to attend or send a representative to this seminar, and while only a few of these responded, it was attended by a wide range of people, many of whom were introduced to the pentecostal movement for the first time. *The National Catholic Reporter, Ave Maria, America* and *Time* ran stories on the seminar which stirred further interest in pentecostal prayer meetings during the summer of 1968.[17]

In the spring of 1968, Father Raymond Cahill, pastor of Our Lady of Mercy Parish in Potomac, Maryland, a Washington suburb, was approached by several of his parishioners who told him of having received the baptism in the Holy Spirit and the gift of tongues. Early in June Father Cahill was persuaded to accompany two of these parishioners, Mrs. Judith Tydings and Sister Mary Alberic, the superior of the generalate of the Sisters of Mercy, along with Sister Charlene, the principal of his parish school, on a visit to Rev. Harald Bredesen, pastor of the First Reformed Church in Mount Vernon, New York. Bredesen prayed with his visitors and Father Cahill and Sister Charlene received the baptism in the Spirit and began to pray in tongues after Bredesen instructed them. Upon returning to Potomac it was decided to hold regular prayer meetings. About 20 people gathered in the basement of the rectory several days later for the first of these. The next week the rectory basement proved to be too small to hold the number that came for the meeting. The following week the meeting was held at night to allow more men to attend, and about 70 came. The week after that 100 were on hand for the meeting, many of them coming from the summer school at the Catholic University of America in Washington.

At this point Father Cahill informed the archbishop of Washington of what was happening and was told not to attend any more meetings or to allow the parish facilities to be used pending further investigation. For the rest of the summer the prayer meetings were held in the homes of various parishioners until they were finally settled in a house maintained by the Fathers of Mercy in nearby Bethesda. Father Cahill was subsequently allowed by his bishop to return to the prayer meetings and was transferred, at his request, to an inner-city parish in southeast Washington. He assisted in the formation of a Catholic pentecostal community among students at Catholic University at the end of the summer of 1969.[18]

In the late spring of 1968, about two weeks before the feast of Pentecost, Mrs. Tydings visited the Trappist monastery at Berryville, Virginia, and gave one of the monks, Father Matthew Killian, some articles on the pentecostal movement. These articles aroused Father Killian's interest and he and several other monks began to pray that they might receive the baptism in the Holy Spirit on the feast of Pentecost. The day of the feast came and nothing happened. The following day Rev. Bob Topping, a pentecostal minister of the Church at Northern Virginia, came to the monastery and prayed with the monks for the baptism in the Spirit. One of the monks spoke in tongues that day and Father Killian received the gift of tongues on the following day.[19] At about the same time, another group of Trappists at a monastery in Ava, Missouri, received the baptism of the Holy Spirit after praying with several faculty members and students from an Assembly of God college in Springfield, Missouri.[20] That same summer another Trappist monk, Father Anthony Delisi of Holy Spirit Abbey in Conyers, Georgia, received the baptism of the Holy Spirit and the gift of tongues while attending summer school at Notre Dame; together with James Byrne and Peter Edwards of the Notre Dame community he introduced the pentecostal movement to the monks at Our Lady of Gethsemani Abbey in Kentucky in August 1968.[21] In

September 1969 Rev. David DuPlessis, an internationally known Pentecostal minister, visited the Trappist abbey of New Clairvaux near Vina, California, at the invitation of one of the monks and introduced them to the pentecostal movement.[22] In October 1969 one of the monks at St. Joseph's Abbey in Spencer, Massachusetts, received the baptism in the Spirit after praying with Father James Powers, S.J., and together with Father Powers led others of the Trappist community at Spencer into the baptism of the Spirit.[23]

In August, 1968 Father Francis MacNutt preached a retreat for priests in the archdiocese of Seattle, Washington, in the course of which he spoke to some of the retreatants about the baptism in the Spirit and the charismatic renewal. Several asked him to pray with them, and they experienced the baptism of the Spirit and spoke in tongues. Father MacNutt introduced these priests to Father Dennis Bennett, an Episcopalian priest and the pastor of St. Luke's Episcopal Church in Seattle, who had been involved in the pentecostal movement since 1959 and had introduced many Roman Catholics to the baptism in the Spirit. With the addition of this core of priests and with the assistance of Father Bennett, several Catholic prayer groups were formed in the state of Washington.[24]

In the same month Mr. and Mrs. John Leary took up residence in Albuquerque, New Mexico, where he was enrolled at the University of Albuquerque. They had moved from Midland, Texas, where they had received the baptism in the Spirit early in 1968 through their landlord and his wife, Baptists and members of the Full Gospel Business Men. The Learys had been instrumental in leading other Catholics in Midland and Odessa, Texas, to receive the baptism in the Spirit. When they arrived in Albuquerque they began to tell others about the charismatic renewal. A Catholic pentecostal community began to take shape which grew within a year to number about 200 people. At one time this community included contingents from Los Alamos, Las Vegas and Santa Fe, New Mexico—all of which eventually withdrew to form communities in their own cities.[25]

Father Blaise Czaia, C.P., and Lawrence Finn, a Passionist seminarian, moved to Louisville, Kentucky, late in the summer of 1968 from Detroit where they had been involved with the Ann Arbor community. A prayer group was formed in the Passionist house of studies in Louisville which was opened to the public later in the fall.[26]

In the fall of 1968 Mrs. Terry Cirner, the sister of Ralph Martin of the Ann Arbor community, was a student at Salve Regina College in Newport, Rhode Island. She began to tell friends there of what was happening at Ann Arbor where she had lived and worked the previous summer. Among those to whom she spoke was a group of Catholics who met irregularly on Sunday afternoons to pray together under the guidance and leadership of Father John Randall, the spiritual director of Our Lady of Providence Seminary in Warwick, Rhode Island. Mrs. Cirner returned to Ann Arbor in February 1969, but the group continued to be moved by her account of the work of the Holy Spirit and by May had determined to pray for the gifts of the Spirit for themselves. One by one the members of the group received the gift of tongues, and by the end of May they had determined to stay and work together throughout the summer.

The Newport group was led in prayer to take up residence in an inner-city neighborhood in the Federal Hill district of Providence, Rhode Island, where apartments, furnishings and food were donated by friends and neighbors. The mornings were spent in prayer and the afternoons and evenings in evangelizing on the streets and through works of mercy. Prayer meetings were begun at Holy Ghost Parish on Monday nights; after several months these were being attended by about 150 people. Soon a second prayer meeting was begun on Thursday nights in one of the apartments. At the end of the summer the group left this neighborhood but the apartment-center was later reopened on a full-time, year-round basis.[27]

Also, in the fall of 1968 Mr. and Mrs. Samuel Hilburn of Chicago, who since June had been attending prayer meetings at St. Benedict's Abbey in Wisconsin, began to gather people in their apartment. From these prayer meetings a community centered in St. Jerome's Parish in Chicago's North Side came into being. At about the same time Father Howard Rafferty, a Carmelite Third Order director, introduced the charismatic renewal to a Third Order chapter in the vicinity of Aylesford, a Carmelite monastery in the western suburbs of Chicago. Weekly prayer meetings were begun which in a few months were attracting crowds of over 100 to the monastery. A third pentecostal community among Chicago Catholics grew out of prayer meetings among a small group of people, most of whom had belonged to charismatic communities in other locales before coming to Chicago. In the following year each of these groups "spun off" several other communities.[28]

1969: The Pastoral Perspective

By the end of 1968 there had been a considerable expansion in the number of people who thought of themselves as Catholic pentecostals, and as the numbers increased, so did the problems. To allow for a sharing of such pastoral wisdom as had been accumulated over the preceding months, the Ann Arbor community, in the first three days of January 1969, was host to a conference for leaders of Catholic pentecostal communities. About 80 people from different parts of the country attended. This was the first national gathering of Catholic pentecostals at which easterners were present in any number.

Among the speakers at this conference were Dr. Robert Frost of Oral Roberts University and Rev. Tommy Tyson, a Methodist minister who had frequently teamed with Father MacNutt to introduce Catholics to the charismatic renewal.

The Third National Catholic Pentecostal Conference was held at Notre Dame on the weekend of April 25–27, 1969 and attracted more than 500 participants from most of the fifty states and from several provinces in Canada. David DuPlessis attended and spoke briefly to those assembled, urging them to be pentecostal within their own Catholic tradition and not to think that they must imitate everything they saw in the pentecostal denominations. Father Graham Pulkingham, the pastor of the Church of the Redeemer, an Episcopal parish in Houston, described what could happen when a whole parish was baptized in the Spirit. Other workshops dealt with other situations in which Christian communities had to be developed.

After the conference the Notre Dame community proposed to set up a Center for Service and Communication which would publish a newsletter, plan national conferences and regional conferences, facilitate communication among prayer groups, and serve as an information center on the charismatic renewal. With the endorsement of many of the leaders of local communities, the center was established on a one-year trial basis at True House in South Bend with James Byrne as coordinator.[29]

The book *Catholic Pentecostals* by Kevin and Dorothy Ranaghan, published by Paulist Press in the spring of 1969, also contributed to the formation of a pastoral perspective by offering an exposition of the development of the movement up to that point and a basic explanation of the charismatic gifts. The capstone to this pastoral thrust came with the adoption by the National Conference of Catholic Bishops at their November meeting of a report prepared by their Committee on Doctrine,

acknowledging that there were legitimate theological reasons and a strong biblical basis for the existence of this
movement. The report recommended that the movement
be allowed to develop and that prudent priests be involved with it.[30]

While these efforts at growth in depth were being
undertaken, the expansion of the movement in numbers
continued unabated. One of those who attended the
Notre Dame conference in April 1969 was Father Harold
Cohen, S.J., the chaplain at Loyola University in New
Orleans. He had read several articles about Catholic involvement in the pentecostal movement but had not met
any Catholics who had experienced the baptism of the
Spirit until early in April when he interviewed a student from Fordham who was seeking admission to the
Society of Jesus. Shortly thereafter, Father Cohen received the baptism in the Spirit and spoke in tongues.
Upon his return from Notre Dame he began to tell
others in New Orleans about what was happening. With
the assistance of Patrick Bourgeois, a member of the
faculty at Loyola who had been part of the Duquesne
group in the spring of 1967, he began prayer meetings
among Catholics in New Orleans in the summer of 1969.
At one of these meetings a woman from Covington,
Louisiana, experienced a healing after being prayed with,
and when she returned to her hometown she told many
Catholics about the charismatic renewal and arranged
for Father Cohen to come to St. Joseph's Abbey, a Benedictine monastery near Covington, and speak to those
Catholics in the neighborhood who were interested. Soon
Catholic pentecostal communities sprang up in Lafayette
and Crowley, Louisiana, and Birmingham, Alabama, as
Catholics in these places heard of what was happening in
New Orleans.[31]

Also present at Notre Dame in April 1969 was Father
Dennis McCarthy, O.M.I., of St. Paul, Minnesota. Father
McCarthy had been active as a retreat master for some

years when, in March 1968, a woman at one of his retreats told him of having received the baptism in the Spirit and speaking in tongues. In the next few months he came into this experience himself, and as he told other Catholics of what had happened to him, a group began to gather around him in the Twin Cities. At a retreat at the Cenacle Retreat House in Wayzata, Minnesota, in January 1969, about 20 of these people received the baptism in the Spirit, and from that time regular prayer meetings were held in the St. Paul-Minneapolis area. In the fall of 1968 Father McCarthy and Reverend Ralph Wilkerson spoke to a group of Catholics and Protestants in Grand Forks, North Dakota, about the charismatic renewal. This proved to be the beginning of an ecumenical pentecostal community in that city.[32]

Growth, in wisdom and in numbers, continued to be a theme and a concern of the Catholic pentecostal movement in 1970. The Ann Arbor Community again hosted a pastoral conference at the beginning of January and over 300 people came, including a large contingent from the south. The Fourth National Conference in South Bend in June drew more than 1,300 people from all parts of the United States and Canada. The Center for Communication and Service, established the previous year on a trial basis, was put on a permanent footing under the direction of a service committee of eight from the midwest who, in turn, were to choose a larger advisory board from among the leaders of Catholic pentecostal communities around the country.[33]

The story of the growing involvement of Catholics in the charismatic renewal over the last few years which is told in the preceding pages is admittedly a sketchy account of what has happened. An essay of this length demanded brevity and generalization and dictated a focus on communities rather than on individuals. Indeed, the peculiar instinct of Catholics who have become involved seems to be to form some sort of community for prayer and life, usually with other Catholics. By no means does the foregoing account mention every locale in which Catholic pentecostals are to be found. Its aim has been to place the events of the spring of 1967 in a larger context and to substantiate the statement of the American bishops that "the pentecostal movement in the Catholic Church is not the acceptance of the ideology or practices of any denomination, but likes to consider itself a renewal in the spirit of the first Pentecost." [34]

Notes

1. The baptism in the Holy Spirit and other expressions used in this chapter are explained elsewhere in this book.
2. Kevin and Dorothy Ranaghan, *Catholic Pentecostals* (New York: Paulist Press, 1969) chapters 1 and 2.
3. The author remembers the following as having been present: James Byrne, James Cavnar, Mr. and Mrs. Paul DeCelles, Peter Edwards, Dr. Josephine Ford, Mr. and Mrs. Bertil Ghezzi, Father Edward O'Connor, C.S.C., Andrew Plodowski, Mr. and Mrs. Kevin Ranaghan, Gerald Rauch and Father Jerome Wilson, C.S.C. from Notre Dame and South Bend; Stephen Clark, Ralph Martin and Mr. and Mrs. Wayne Wood from Michigan State and Lansing; Robert Morris and Father Kenneth Sommers, S.M., from Cleveland. This list is by no means complete.
4. Mike Smith, "Spiritualists Claim 'Gift of Tongues' at Exorcism Rites," *The Observer* (Notre Dame), I, 10 (April 13, 1967).
   Dan Murray, "As the Devil Left, I Smelt Clearly the Odor of Burning Sulphur," *Scholastic* (Notre Dame), CIX (April 14, 1967), pp. 18–20.
   "Notre Dame Priests and Students Hold Pentecostal Prayer Meetings," *National Catholic Reporter*, April 19, 1967.
   Robert Wonderly, Jr., "Pentecostals at Notre Dame Are Not Sweeping Campus, Chaplain Advises," *Our Sunday Visitor*, May 14, 1967.
   Edward O'Connor, C.S.C., "A Catholic Pentecostal Movement," *Ave Maria*, CV, 22 (June 3, 1967), pp. 6–10.
   Henri Nouwen, "A Critical Analysis," *Ave Maria*, CV, 22 (June 3, 1967), pp. 13ff.

5. Kevin and Dorothy Ranaghan, *op. cit.*, pp. 97–106.
6. Interview with Nadine A. Nader, March 31, 1970.
   Michael Fitzgerald, *Questionnaire*. (Much of the information for this chapter was obtained from a questionnaire sent out by the author in February and March, 1970. Henceforth, this will be referred to as *Quest*.)
7. Rev. Edward Keefe, *Quest*.
   Brother Walter Schoenberg, O.C.S.O., *Quest*.
   Rev. Samuel Davis, O.C.S.O., *Quest*.
8. Rev. Charles Harris, C.S.C., *Quest*.
   Harvey Gebhart, *Quest*.
9. Kevin and Dorothy Ranaghan, *op. cit.*, p. 50.
10. Interview with Rev. Francis MacNutt, O.P., Dec. 13, 1969.
    Stephen Darst, "Pentecostalism Comes In from the Tents," *St. Louis Review*, Aug. 29, 1969.
    Rev. Francis MacNutt, O.P., letter to the author, June 3, 1970.
11. Tape by Rev. Daniel Scully, O.S.B.
12. *Ibid.*
    Tape by Sister Marie Catherine Olinger, O.P.
13. Theodore Sohn, *Quest*.
    Daniel Giordano, *Quest*.
    Rev. James Powers, S.J., *Quest*. and comments at Ann Arbor Leaders' Conference, Jan. 1, 1969.
14. Bertil Ghezzi, *The Days of Renewal in Michigan*, mimeographed publication, Dec. 1969.
15. *Michigan Days of Renewal: Pastoral Newsletter*, April 1969; March 1970.
16. Kevin and Dorothy Ranaghan, *op. cit.*, pp. 51–55.
17. *National Catholic Reporter*, June 12, 1968.
    James F. Powers, S.J., "Catholic Pentecostals," *America*, July 20, 1968.
    Ken Peters, "When the Spirit Moves You," *Ave Maria*, Aug. 17, 1968.
    Time, "Charisma on the Rise," June 14, 1968.
18. Interviews with Mrs. Edith Difato, Dec. 23, 1969, and Father Raymond Cahill, Dec. 27, 1969.
    Mrs. Judith Tydings, *Quest*.
19. Mrs. Judith Tydings, *Quest*.
    Rev. Matthew Killian, O.C.S.O., "Pentecost and the Paschal Mystery," *Voice*, XVIII, 3 (April 1970), pp. 13ff.
20. Rev. Samuel Dennis, O.C.S.O., *Quest*.
21. Rev. Anthony Delisi, O.C.S.O., *Quest*.
22. Rev. Francis X. Davis, O.C.S.O., *Quest*.
23. Rev. Basil Pennington, O.C.S.O., *Quest*.
24. Interview with Rev. Francis MacNutt, O.P., Dec. 13, 1969.

Rev. George McLean, "Priest Discounts Seattle's 'Tongues' Vogue," *The Progress* (Seattle, Wash.), Oct. 18, 1968.

Rev. James Eblen, "Bible Cites 'Gift of Tongues'," *ibid.*, Oct. 25, 1968.

Rev. Earl LaBerge, "Readers Lash Author of 'Tongues' Story," *ibid.*, Oct. 25, 1968.

25. Interview with Dennis Yule, August 5, 1969.
John Leary, *Quest.*

26. John Meehan, "Pentecostal Group Grows Quietly Here," *The Record* (Louisville, Ky.), Oct. 23, 1969.
Bro. Lawrence Finn, C.P., *Quest.*
Richard Hughes, C.P., *Quest.*

27. Russell Kirk, unpublished history of the Catholic pentecostal community in Providence, 1969.
Rev. John Randall, *Quest.*

28. Interview with Mr. and Mrs. Samuel Hilburn, July 29, 1969.
Rev. Howard Rafferty, O. Carm., talk given at St. Benedict's Abbey, Benet Lake, Wisc., June 1969.

29. Kevin M. Ranaghan for the Notre Dame Community, "A Proposal for a Center of Service and Communication".

30. *Report of the Committee on Doctrine of the National Conference of Catholic Bishops Submitted to the Bishops in Their Meeting in Washington, D.C., Nov. 14, 1969.* Press Dept., U. S. Catholic Conference, Washington, D.C.

31. Rev. Harold Cohen, S.J., Newsletters to friends, June, July, August, 1969. "Impressions of the Notre Dame Conference on Charismatic Renewal, April 25–27, 1969" (for private circulation only), 1969.

32. Rev. Dennis McCarthy, O.M.I., *Quest.* Letter to the author, Sept. 15, 1969.

33. The Service Committee in June 1970 consisted of James Byrne, Father Edward O'Connor, C.S.C., and Kevin Ranaghan of South Bend, Ind., George Martin of Lansing, Mich., Ralph Martin and Stephen Clark of Ann Arbor, Mich., Father George Kosicki, C.S.B., of Detroit, and Bertil Ghezzi of Grand Haven, Mich.

34. *Report of the Committee on Doctrine of the National Conference of Catholic Bishops Submitted to the Bishops in Their Meeting in Washington, D.C., Nov. 14, 1969.* Press Dept., U. S. Catholic Conference, Washington, D.C.

Charismatic Renewal and the Church of Tomorrow

George Martin

The beginning of the charismatic renewal of the Catholic Church in 1967 was, to say the least, unexpected. It was not something that was programmed or planned; it was not something we had been warned about or were looking forward to. It came with the unexpectedness which often characterizes God's actions breaking into our midst.

The growth of the charismatic renewal since 1967 has been no less surprising. The number of men and women involved has risen steadily and dramatically. Even more significant has been the growth in maturity and holiness of those involved. Many movements and causes have expanded rapidly; many have also withered away just as rapidly because they lacked a firm foundation. If the experience of the last three years is any indication, the charismatic renewal promises to be much more than just a passing fad in the life of the Church.

It is difficult to predict what the Church of tomorrow will look like. We need only compare the Church of 1950 with the Church of today to realize that she is in a time of rapid change. We know that the core of the Christian message is unchanging—Christ has died, Christ is risen, Christ will come again. But as we move farther from the core, change becomes possible, and even inevitable. The eternal message of salvation must be expressed in the words of today and find expression in life today. Tomorrow's language and life will almost certainly be different.

If it is difficult to trace the contours of the Church of tomorrow, it is even more difficult to predict what impact the charismatic renewal will have on the Church of tomorrow. If the charismatic renewal were merely the work of man, some projections could be made, graphs of growth plotted out and a report nicely drawn up. However, since the charismatic renewal is not the simple result of human thought and effort (however much these may affect it), its future ultimately does not lie in men's hands. God spoke through Isaiah: "As the heavens are higher than the earth, so are my ways higher than your ways, and my thoughts than your thoughts" (Is. 55, 9). If ever caution was necessary in forecasting the future, it is with regard to the charismatic renewal of the Catholic Church.

But forecast we must. We are better able to respond to the guidance of the Holy Spirit if we have some insight into the course of his action, into the direction that he is trying to lead us. Willfully ignoring the signs of the times is rarely a mark of docility to God. Ignorance, however blissful, is not blessed.

What then do the signs of the times indicate, however tentatively? What hints and glimpses can we make out of the future—of a Church in change and a movement under the impetus of the Holy Spirit?

One mark of change is that it often counts for very little. "The more things change, the more they remain the same." Or applying this to the Church: The more we go about the work of renewal, the more we find out how difficult true renewal is, how hard significant and positive progress is to come by.

The object of liturgical renewal is the renewal of the Christian community at prayer together. But it is far easier to juggle rubrics than to really renew our community prayer. The changes introduced into the Mass were necessary and are helpful. But they are only helpful. They are not the goal in themselves. Changes in the form of prayer do not guarantee a renewal in our life of prayer, although they should aid it. When the Mass was put into English, many people found out that they simply didn't know how to pray in English either.

On another level, the creation of parish councils is a recent and widespread event in the Church. One source estimates that one half of the parishes in the United States now have parish councils. There are good and compelling reasons for parish councils. But it may be wondered if their existence necessarily guarantees a significantly improved state of affairs. In theory, they should help to accomplish the mission of Christ today; in practice, they have been known merely to perpetuate the type of parish operation that held reign for decades before they were created. All too often they have had minimal effect in actually renewing their parishes.

More and more, laymen are moving into significant roles of service to the Church. I welcome this development; I am a part of it. But there is nothing magical about having a layman perform a job which was previously done by a priest or religious. We laymen can be every bit as incompetent as the worst imaginable cleric. If receiving holy orders does not automatically guarantee spiritual vision and depth, neither does not receiving holy orders. For both priests and laity, the process of growth into spiritual maturity and leadership can be a painfully slow one.

Fundamental Renewal of the Church

In short, it is far easier to change forms and faces, drop practices and juggle structures, than it is to actually build up the body of Christ. All our human efforts are necessary—but a good deal more than human effort is necessary. "Unless the Lord build the house, those who build it labor in vain," teaches Psalm 127. I believe that the charismatic renewal is an attempt by God to effect a fundamental renewal within the Catholic Church. It appears to be the Holy Spirit bringing about the renewal that Vatican Council II called for, and that all our human efforts are straining at.

The Spirit gives us life. And *only* the Spirit gives life. The renewal that is taking place in the hearts of men through the charismatic renewal is an experience of the life-giving Spirit, of the abundant life promised by Jesus, of the Father's love. When this life is actually experienced, then the forms which manifest this life become meaningful. Without the underlying life, the forms become dead—however valid or renewed they might be.

The Gloria that is said at Mass is a very simple example of this. For all too many people, it is a prayer that is said because the missal includes it. The priest starts it and the people in the pews repeat it. But its expressions of praise of God, whether they be worded "We give you thanks for your great glory!" or "We praise you for your glory!" have little meaning for many. And how could they—unless a person has some knowledge, some taste, some experience of the glory of God—a knowledge or taste or experience which does evoke thanksgiving?

I do not mean to say that every prayer should be an emotional one. I do mean to say that often we barely mean the prayers we find ourselves saying. Good intentions alone cannot overcome this. We must have some experience of that about which we speak and pray before we can advance far beyond the formal mouthing of words. We must feel some personal gratitude to God before our prayers of thanksgiving are truly thanks-giving.

Most often the words we pray are the correct words. Exchanging them for a different set of words won't help that much. But experiencing the reality behind them can bring them alive. Living the life that they are meant to formalize and express can make them once again a meaningful expression.

Christianity did not begin as a set of precisely worded doctrines and as a well-thought-out structure. It began with a Person, Jesus of Nazareth who is the Christ. It continued through individuals coming to experience and live the life of his Spirit, the Holy Spirit. A renewal of the life of the Church must begin with a renewal of individual lives in his Spirit.

The charismatic renewal promises to be such a renewal for the Church of tomorrow. It promises to be a vehicle whereby the Holy Spirit can accomplish the fundamental renewal of Christian lives which is necessary for the renewal of the Church. It can be a means whereby the life of faith of the entire Church is strengthened.

It is becoming more evident every day that the Catholic Church in America is in a time of crisis. This crisis is earmarked by an atmosphere of confusion and uncertainty, by widespread discouragement fading into apathy, by bitterness on the part of many. There seems to have been a considerable loss of hope and nerve— and, underlying all these symptoms, a considerable loss of faith. The crisis of the Church today is, at its roots, a crisis of faith.

Respectable scholars are calling these days "the darkest hour" of the Catholic Church in America, and they are warning that we are on the brink of revolution. How accurate their assessments and forecasts are is a matter of opinion. It seems clear, however, that the present turmoil in the Church is a matter of serious concern. It seems also clear that the situation will not significantly improve unless some solution is found to the basic cause of the turmoil, the crisis of faith.

The charismatic renewal is first of all a renewal of

faith—a renewal holding out promise of answering the crisis of faith in the Church today. It is a renewal of men's lives with God—which is to say the life of the Holy Spirit in man. It is a renewal proceeding from an experience of the reality and greatness of God, a renewal which finds its natural outcome in a renewal of an individual's prayer life.

Faith and prayer are intimately connected. The life of faith cannot be sustained without prayer, and prayer cannot be sustained without faith. Many in the Catholic Church today are echoing the words of the apostles, "Lord, teach us how to pray." It is not technique that they are looking for, but a sense of the presence of God and the nearness of God, and a strong sense and faith that their heavenly Father is indeed a Person who does hear and answer prayer. It is difficult to speak to someone who is absent. The charismatic renewal has given many persons the conviction that God is not dead or absent or indifferent, but near and loving.

It would be a mistake to characterize the charismatic renewal merely as a renewal of an individual's personal relationship with God. It may be this first of all, but at the same time it is a renewal of Christian community, a building up of the body of Christ. As Vatican Council II stated so clearly: "It has pleased God, however, to make men holy and save them not merely as individuals without any mutual bonds, but by making them into a single people, a people which acknowledges him in truth and serves him in holiness." The development of Christian community has been as remarkable a fruit of the charismatic renewal as has been the renewal of individual lives.

The Renewal of Communities

From the very beginnings of the charismatic renewal in 1967, the work of the Spirit has been to gather men and women together in the name of Christ. The "prayer meeting" became the focal structure of the charismatic renewal: Christians coming together to give praise and worship to the Father. It was most often in the context of a prayer meeting that people were introduced into a fuller life in the Holy Spirit. From one point of view, the charismatic renewal could have been considered a movement of prayer meetings.

Within the last months, however, a further development may be noticed. As prayer groups have become larger and matured, they have increasingly become real Christian communities. They are not merely incidental gatherings of a number of people once a week for prayer; they are growing into stable fellowships wherein men and women can find an overall context for their Christian lives. I do not mean that "underground churches" are being formed. Nor do I mean that ghettos are being created to provide an escape from the world. Rather, within the institutional Catholic Church, communities of the faithful are growing up. The communities may find their base in an individual parish, or may draw their members from several parishes in one city. There may be various sub-groupings within the community, including groups oriented toward social action. But all have the earmarks of genuine community. They are not just "one more meeting" that people try to fit into their lives. They are the center of gravity for the lives of people as members of the body of Christ. They are very concrete manifestations of the fact that we are called to the Father together, that we are called to him as members of his people.

Since Vatican Council II, the cry for the formation of Christian communities has grown ever louder. The charismatic renewal has evolved to lead in the formation of such communities. If in the earliest days it seemed as if being baptized in the Holy Spirit was the beginning and end of what God had in mind, this is clearly no longer the case. Being baptized in the Holy Spirit is now better understood as an initiation into a fuller Christian life, and of necessity a fuller Christian life with others. The Spirit of Christ works in our lives to lead us to the Father; at the same time the Spirit forms us together as a people on pilgrimage to the Father.

The communal dimension of the charismatic renewal is further brought out by reflecting on what is most strikingly different and unique about the charismatic renewal. It is clearly the exercise of the charisms of the Holy Spirit—the gifts of the Holy Spirit listed by St. Paul. These gifts are given for the good of the community. They are given for use within the community to build it up as the body of Christ—such is the teaching of St. Paul, St. Thomas Aquinas, and St. John of the Cross.

If the charisms are given for the building up of Christian community, a mature community also enables the exercise of the charisms to have its greatest effect. While the charisms can in one sense be exercised in the midst of any gathering of Christians, it is only in the context of an established Christian community that they can play their most proper role.

There is a difference between the two lists St. Paul gives of the workings of the Holy Spirit in Chapter 12 of 1 Corinthians. His first listing is of gifts: "One may have the gift of preaching with wisdom . . . another the gift of healing, through this one Spirit; one, the power of miracles, another, prophecy. . . ." (1 Cor. 12, 8–10). The second list, however, is not of gifts or charisms, but of offices and ministries within the Christian community: "In the Church, God has given the first place to apostles, the second to prophets, the third to teachers; after them, workers of miracles, then healers, helpers, administrators. . . ." (1 Cor. 12, 28).

As charismatic Christian communities have matured, individuals have matured within them in their different roles of service. Some have been equipped to perform the works of teaching and leadership—and have developed into the acknowledged teachers and leaders of the community. Others have received gifts of prophecy or discernment—and have matured into performing these functions within the community on a consistent basis.

So too for the various other roles necessary for the life of the Christian community, whether spiritual or administrative. Laymen and laywomen are maturing in their development and exercise of the gifts which they have received for the building up of the body of Christ.

A Fuller Apostolate

The question of the relationship between these charismatic "ministries" exercised by laymen and the ordained priesthood is too large a question for this chapter to address adequately. It is clear that the charismatic ministries do not replace the ordained ministry; priests need not worry about becoming obsolete. Rather, just the opposite seems to be occurring.

During the centuries before Vatican Council II, members of the Church generally fell into two rather neat categories. There were the clergy, and there were the laity. (There were also religious—a kind of mini-clergy.) The clergy pretty well ran things; if you were a member of the laity, your role in the Church was generally quite passive.

Change began to occur around the beginning of the century, largely due to the efforts of Pope Pius X. The notion of "Catholic Action" developed—the "participation of the laity in the apostolate of the hierarchy." Laymen could become active in the Church, but as "helpers" to the clergy in "their" apostolate.

During the 1940's, the idea of the "apostolate of the laity" grew. Here the accent was on laymen and laywomen performing an apostolate that was particularly their own. The laity were no longer helpers in "someone else's" apostolate; they had their own proper contribution to make to the advancing of the kingdom of God.

While both "Catholic Action" and the "lay apostolate" were important historical advances, they were not totally satisfactory answers to the needs of the Church. Both movements grew out of a view which over-emphasized the clergy/laity dichotomy. What was common to the call of both clergy and laity was often overlooked; attention was instead focused on their differences. Catholic Action often degenerated into a fleeing of the world for service in the sanctuary. The lay apostolate went to the other pole, and largely limited its vision of the apostolate to those areas where priests weren't in theory supposed to tread—political involvement, social action, building the earth.

Because these views of the apostolate focused too heavily either on what was the priest's *exclusive* role or on what was the layman's *exclusive* role, their *common* apostolate was very often overlooked. The work of building Christian communities suffered, because Christian communities cannot be formed by the work of either clergy or laity alone. And there was often very little working together.

The charismatic renewal of the Church holds promise for a much more balanced state of affairs. The maturing of the charismatic ministries holds promise of a fuller involvement of every member of the Church in building up the body of Christ without jeopardizing anyone's role. It holds this promise because its primary focus is not on the differences between clergy and laity, but on the gifts of service that every follower of Christ receives.

Since Vatican Council II, the call has been for "co-responsibility" in the Church. There is an increasing demand for new structures—structures which will allow every Christian to exercise his co-responsibility for the work of Christ. But new structures are only a part of the need. Christians need to grow into their more active roles if co-responsibility is to be more than a dream. New structures don't guarantee this growth; being elected to a council doesn't automatically give one greater spiritual vision and maturity.

Neither, certainly, does involvement in the charismatic renewal guarantee spiritual vision and maturity. But it is through the charismatic renewal that many men and women are receiving and developing gifts of service for the community. And it is within charismatic communities that a great deal of "co-responsibility" for the work of Christ has already been achieved.

If the observations presented above are correct, then there is a congruence between what the charismatic renewal has to offer the Church and the needs of the Church highlighted by Vatican Council II:

The basic crisis the Church is going through today is a crisis of faith—and the charismatic renewal is first of all a renewal of faith.

The call today is for Christian community and co-responsibility—and the charismatic renewal is finding its center of gravity in the formation of Christian communities and the development of roles of service within them.

Faith, community, service—these are the timeless needs of the Church, and the areas in which the Church always stands in need of renewal and upbuilding. They are at once gifts of God and the work of men, the response of men. The charismatic renewal is a work of the Holy Spirit, giving faith and calling forth faith, creating Christian community and equipping men and women for ministry.

The future of the charismatic renewal within the Catholic Church, then, would appear to be a charismatically renewed Catholic Church.

I believe that the charismatic renewal can be the vehicle whereby the life of the entire Catholic Church will be renewed. I believe that its potential is not merely to be a movement or a sect within the Church—a specialized Department of Spiritual Experiences off in one corner—but to infuse and renew the entire Church.

Perhaps a comparison can be made with the liturgical movement. The goal of those engaged in the work of liturgical renewal was not to create a separate movement within the Church and enjoy quality liturgies among themselves; their goal was to renew the liturgical life of the entire Church. In order to accomplish this goal, it was necessary for the liturgical movement to have some organization and identity as a definite movement. Since the enactment of liturgical reforms by Vatican Council II, however, the identity of the liturgical movement as a movement has all but vanished.

It is in this sense that the charismatic renewal can be considered a movement—a Catholic pentecostal movement. The goal is a charismatically renewed Church, not a separate "pentecostal" organization "for people who go for that sort of thing." Having some identity as a movement may be necessary for a time in order to accomplish the larger goal. But the larger goal is the significant one: a charismatically renewed Catholic Church.

I am not concerned to predict what the sociological shape of the Catholic Church of tomorrow will be, nor how many members or priests or religious she will have, nor what cultural forms her life of worship will take. These matters are admittedly important. But what is of greater importance is whether the Church of tomorrow will have traveled further on her pilgrimage to the Father —whether a spiritual renewal will have taken place. What is decisive to the Church is the haunting question of Christ: "When the Son of Man comes, will he find faith on earth?" (Lk. 18, 8).

By focusing on the level of spiritual renewal—renewal in faith, community and service—I do not mean to minimize or overlook the specifically "pentecostal" contributions the charismatic renewal can make to the life of the Church. As one of my friends remarked, we should expect to see the day when our popes and bishops perform miracles, as we pray for them to do when they are consecrated, or when they are guided by prophecies and visions, as popes and bishops have been in times past. Miracles and prophecies, as well as sacraments and authority, are means toward deepening the life of the Spirit within us. But it is the life of the Holy Spirit within us and within the Church which is of ultimate importance. And it is this life—within us and within the Church—which the same Holy Spirit is charismatically renewing today.

It remains for us to be faithful to him. God's plan does not unfold by necessity but through the free response of man. In St. Paul's term, it is possible to quench the Spirit. It is possible to frustrate or sidetrack the renewal of the Church that God is offering today. Christ's words concerning the different responses given to John the Baptist's message hold no less true in our time: "All the people who heard him, and the tax collectors too, acknowledged God's plan by accepting baptism from John; but by refusing baptism from him, the Pharisees and the lawyers had thwarted what God had in mind for them" (Lk. 7, 29–30).

Whether the charismatic renewal within the Church will bear fruit in a charismatically renewed Catholic Church will depend on the leading of the Holy Spirit and our faithfulness. The signs of the times indicate that this is the direction that he is leading us in, that this is what he wishes to accomplish. Our concern must be to be guided by him, to follow his paths in his time, to proceed on as the Spirit leads us.

Notes on the Contributors

KEVIN M. RANAGHAN was born in New York City and attended school there, taking his bachelor's degree in philosophy at St. Joseph's College. He subsequently went on to graduate work in theology at the University of Notre Dame, and for a time was an instructor in theology at St. Mary's College. He has spoken before groups of Catholic and Protestant pentecostals in many parts of the United States and Canada.

DOROTHY RANAGHAN is a native of Pittsburgh who graduated from Duquesne University there in 1964. She received an M.A. degree in theology from Notre Dame and has been a high school religion teacher. Mrs. Ranaghan has two children and is an instructor in Lamaze childbirth classes in South Bend, Ind.

STEPHEN B. CLARK is a graduate of Yale (1962), a former Fulbright scholar in Germany, and the holder of an M.A. degree in philosophy from Notre Dame. For five years ending in 1970 he was a national staff member of the Cursillo Movement, and he still serves that group as research director. He is on the staff of St. Mary's Student Parish at the University of Michigan and is coordinator of the charismatic community at Ann Arbor.

JAMES CAVNAR took his B.A. degree in theology at Notre Dame in 1967 and has been the leader of the Ann Arbor charismatic prayer meeting for three years. Both he and his wife, Betsy, are musicians.

SUSAN B. ANTHONY, a great-niece of the 19th-century suffragette leader, is the author of four books resulting from her experiences as a journalist and as a theologian. She holds a Ph.D. degree in theology from St. Mary's College and has taught theology at Marymount College, Boca Raton, Fla. Her latest book, *The Ghost in My Life,* is an autobiography (Chosen Books, Inc.).

LEON KORTENKAMP is chairman of the art department at Penn High School, Mishawaka, Ind. He graduated from Loras College, Dubuque, served two years in the Navy, and went on to graduate work in the fine arts at Notre Dame.

VIRGINIA KORTENKAMP graduated from St. Mary's College and has served as one of the leaders of the South Bend Cursillo Movement. She and her husband have three sons, Paul, Mark, and John.

RALPH MARTIN, after graduating *magna cum laude* in philosophy from Notre Dame in 1964, went on to study at Princeton with a Woodrow Wilson Fellowship. He later gave that up to devote himself to full-time apostolic work in the campus ministry at Ann Arbor. He was on the national research staff of the Cursillo Movement from 1965 to 1970. He and his wife, Anne, have one son, John, born in 1970.

BERTIL W. GHEZZI earned his B.A. degree in history from Duquesne in 1963 and his Ph.D. from Notre Dame in 1969. He is currently an assistant professor of history at Grand Valley State College, Allendale, Mich. He and his wife, Mary Lou, have four children.

JAMES E. BYRNE is doing full-time apostolic work on the campus at Notre Dame, where in 1968 he graduated with a degree in history. He is national coordinator of the

Communications Center for the Charismatic Renewal, which maintains its headquarters in South Bend.

JAMES CONNELLY, C.S.C., was ordained a priest of the Congregation of the Holy Cross in 1964, after studying at Notre Dame and at the Gregorian University in Rome. He is presently a graduate student in the history of Christianity at the University of Chicago Divinity School.

GEORGE MARTIN has graduated from St. Mary's College, Winona, Minn., and from Notre Dame, where he won his Ph.D. in philosophy in 1969. He went on to become assistant superintendent for continuing education for the diocese of Lansing, Mich. He and his wife, Mary, and their four children, have recently moved to Tulsa, Okla., where he has a similar position with the Oklahoma City-Tulsa diocese.

Suggested Readings

GENERAL REFERENCE BOOKS

W. Abbott (ed.), *The Documents of Vatican II* (New York, 1966).
R. Brown *et al.* (eds.), *The Jerome Biblical Commentary* (Englewood Cliffs, N.J., 1968).
J. Clarkson *et al.* (eds.), *The Church Teaches* (St. Louis, 1955).
F. Cross (ed.), *The Oxford Dictionary of the Christian Church* (London, 1957).

SCRIPTURE STUDIES

B. Anderson, *Understanding the Old Testament* (Englewood Cliffs, N.J., 1966).
C. Charlier, *The Christian Approach to the Bible* (Westminster, Md., 1958).
L. Grollenberg, *A New Look at an Old Book* (Paramus, N.J., 1969).
J. McKenzie, *The Power and the Wisdom* (Milwaukee, 1965).
———, *The Two-Edged Sword* (Milwaukee, 1956).

LITURGICAL STUDIES

L. Bouyer, *Liturgical Piety* (Notre Dame, 1955).
I. Dalmais, *Introduction to the Liturgy* (Baltimore, 1961).
C. Davis, *Liturgy and Doctrine* (New York, 1961).
A. Martimort (ed.), *The Church at Prayer* (New York, 1969).

CHRISTIAN SPIRITUALITY

S. Anthony, *The Prayer-Supported Apostle* (Notre Dame, 1965).

L. Bouyer, *Introduction to Spirituality* (New York, 1961).
D. Gee, *Concerning Spiritual Gifts* (Springfield, Mo., 1937).
———, *Fruitful or Barren?* (Springfield, Mo., 1937).
H. Graef, *Mystics of Our Times* (Garden City, N.Y., 1962).
W. Inge, *Christian Mysticism* (London, 1921).
H. Martin (ed.), *The Interior Castle of St. Theresa of Avila* (Garden City, N.Y., 1956).
E. Peers (ed.), *Ascent of Mount Carmel by St. John of the Cross* (Garden City, N.Y., 1958).
E. Underhill, *The Spiritual Life* (London, *n.d.*).

ECUMENICAL DIMENSIONS OF THE CHARISMATIC REVIVAL

P. Damboriena, *Tongues as of Fire* (Washington, D.C., 1969).
D. Du Plessis, *The Spirit Bade Me Go* (Dallas, 1961).
K. Kendrick, *The Promise Fulfilled: A History of the American Pentecostal Movement* (Springfield, Mo., 1961).
J. Nichol, *Pentecostalism* (New York, 1966).
J. Sherrill, *They Speak with Other Tongues* (New York, 1965).
D. Wilkerson, *The Cross and the Switchblade* (New York, 1964).